Recipe for
change

A good practice guide
to school meals

Edited by
Carrieanne Hurley and Ashley Riley

CPAG • 94 White Lion Street • London N1 9PF

CPAG promotes action for the relief, directly or indirectly, of poverty among children and families with children. We work to ensure that those on low incomes get their full entitlements to welfare benefits. In our campaigning and information work we seek to improve benefits and policies for low-income families in order to eradicate the injustice of poverty. If you are not already supporting us, please consider making a donation, or ask for details of our membership schemes and publications.

Poverty Publication 112

Published by CPAG
94 White Lion Street, London N1 9PF

© CPAG 2004

ISBN 1 901698 61 0

A CIP record for this book is available from the British Library

Every effort has been made to trace copyright holders and to obtain their permission for the use of photographs in this book. Any omissions are entirely unintentional. Details of any acknowledgements that should be incorporated in future reprints or editions of this book should be addressed to CPAG.

Cover and design by Devious Designs 0114 275 5634
Typeset by Boldface 020 7833 8868
Printed by Russell Press 0115 978 4505
Cover photo reproduced with permission of reportdigital.co.uk (photographer: Paul Carter)

Contents

Part three: Recommendations

Acknowledgements

We would like to thank everyone who has worked on school meals for CPAG in the past. Particular thanks go to Will McMahon and Tim Marsh, the authors of *Filling the Gap*, for their research into the history of school meals. We are also grateful to Paul Dornan and David Bull for reading an early draft and making useful comments.

Thanks to Alison Key for her commitment and hard work, and for making our idea a reality; and to Pauline Phillips for getting the text to the printers. We would also like to thank Paula McDiarmid for proofreading the text.

We are particularly grateful to The New Deal for Communities in the London Borough of Newham for their financial support.

Ashley would like to thank all his family, friends and colleagues, especially his wife, Sharon, who has endured his excitement and daily worry about completing this project for almost two years.

Carrieanne would like to thank all her colleagues at the London Borough of Newham Education Department, and at West Ham and Plaistow NDC. Thanks to all the school cooks in Newham for their constant hard work and dedication to give our children healthy and nutritious meals every school day; also to the pupils at the schools who stay for a school lunch and those who now will want to. Then last, but by no means least, thanks go to her own children Lisa and Jodie and her very significant other, Nick, who will be relieved that this book is now complete.

Finally, we are enormously grateful to our contributors, who have inspired us with their work, and to the children in all the schools we visited with whom we shared a school meal.

About the authors

Kate Bowie is responsible for the development and implementation of the Grab 5! Project at Sustain, the alliance for better food and farming.

John Dickie is Head of CPAG in Scotland.

Mary Glew is a councillor and Portfolio Holder for Learning on Kingston upon Hull City Council.

Carrieanne Hurley was formerly the New Deal for Communities Healthy Futures Co-ordinator. She is now an independent Food Consultant.

Kay Knight is Head of Traded and Support Services at South Gloucestershire Council.

George McNamara is the Public Policy Officer at NCH children's charity.

David Parry is Head of Operations, Direct and Care Services, Glasgow City Council.

Ashley Riley is CPAG's Press and Parliamentary Officer.

Richard Siddall is responsible for the development and implementation of the Grab 5! Project at Sustain, the alliance for better food and farming.

Ed Yeates is the Headteacher at the Venerable Bede Church of England (Aided) Secondary School, Sunderland.

Foreword

I welcome the Child Poverty Action Group's continuing efforts to eradicate poverty among children and families.

The Government attaches the greatest importance to what a child eats and drinks while at school. That is why the Department for Education and Skills has been working to promote health messages, and educate children and young people so that they are able to make healthy eating choices.

I agree with the finding in *Recipe for Change* that the key to getting pupils to make healthy choices is the widespread adoption of a whole school approach to healthier eating and drinking. In order to help schools achieve this, the Government will shortly be launching an action plan and complementary website that will give schools, and others, the tools they need to implement changes. This good practice guide will make a real practical difference.

Stephen Twigg, Parliamentary Under Secretary of State for Schools at the Department for Education and Skills

Introduction

Carrieanne Hurley and Ashley Riley

One of the key ways in which we can make the issue of child poverty of interest to the general public is to grab the attention of the modern media. The fundamental aim of the Child Poverty Action Group is to raise the profile of child poverty and its realities as a platform from which to campaign to end child poverty. Delivering this message via the media, however, is a challenge, as we recognise that the fact that millions of mothers go without food[1] or that 80 per cent of Pakistani children in the UK live in income poverty does not generally sell newspapers.[2]

When CPAG speaks at national, regional or local level, however, one issue which does receive significant interest is school meals. This coming together of general and media interest in a serious social policy concern is encouraging, and headlines such as 'School Meal Battles' and 'Experts Claim Free School Meals Can Save Lives' show that editors believe that the state of our children's diets does in fact sell newspapers.[3]

Like many issues in the media, school meals are all too often portrayed in a negative light: 'School Meals are Muck' and 'Children Throw Away Their Lunch' are recent examples.[4] The public would be forgiven for thinking that it is all doom and gloom.

There is, of course, bad practice. For example, a recent Soil Association report found that, on average, 35p a head is spent on school meals compared with the 60p a head the Government currently spends on prison food.[5] But there is also good news to share.

An increasing number of schools (some of which appear in this book) are pioneering improvements in the quality of school meals and in the take-up of free school meals. It is concerning that they are able to do this not because of the system, but in spite of it. Yes, the Government has set minimum nutritional guidelines.[6] Yes, the number of children entitled to free school meals has increased by approximately 75,000 since the introduction of the new child tax credit. But there has, to date, been no opportunity for schools to share their good practice and to learn from each other. That is why we are publishing this book.

Recipe for Change: a good practice guide to school meals begins by examining the link between poverty and nutrition. We then review the history of school meals and the campaign work that has been undertaken in this area. The main body of the book focuses on the examples from across Britain of innovative projects that are making a real difference to the provision of school meals.

Our wish would be to see a Britain where every child receives a free school meal. A universal service providing every child in the country with a daily, nutritious school meal would play a major role in addressing health inequalities and producing healthy adults of tomorrow. While we continue to campaign for this end, we, of course, have to review the current system and judge where improvements can be made.

We hope that the wonderful initiatives described in *Recipe for Change: a good practice guide* to school meals will inspire schools, local authorities, decision makers and others to seek to improve school meal provision and increase take-up, and thus make a real difference to our children's lives.

Notes

1   L Platt, *Parallel Lives: poverty among ethnic groups in Britain*, Child Poverty Action Group, 2002

2   Department for Work and Pensions, *Households Below Average Incomes 1994/95-2002/03*, Corporate Document Services, 2004, p59, table 4.7

3   *Kilsyth Chronicle*, 8 May 2002; *Sunday Herald*, 16 June 2002

4   Soil Association, *Food for Life*, Soil Association, 2003

5   See note 4

6   Department for Education and Skills, *National Nutritional Standards for School Lunches*, 2001 at http://www.dfes.gov.uk/schoollunches/juniors.shtml

Part one
School meals and child poverty

One
Poverty and nutrition
George McNamara

When shopping for food the purchaser is presented with a wide variety of products. In fact, those with the money to spend are spoilt for choice. Supermarkets offer different kinds of meat, vegetables and fruit from all over the world. Choices are made on whether to buy organic, free-range, gluten and lactose-free or low-fat products, as well as choosing a preferred brand – an experience unimaginable just a generation ago. Yet, whilst this may describe the shopping experience of families on middle and higher incomes, it does not hold for those less well off. For many families living on low incomes in Britain, their food choices are severely restricted and revolve around deciding between value and own brands, hunting out special offers and looking for clearance-priced goods. The thought of paying extra for better quality, healthier alternatives is a distant dream, likely to be sacrificed for more directly pressing concerns.

The fact that some families in today's Britain, the fourth largest economy in the world, do not have enough to eat or are unable to afford a healthy diet is difficult to comprehend. Often when we hear about food poverty we immediately cast our minds to the poorer countries in the developing world. We think about starvation and famine. But there is also poverty nearer to home. One only has to visit our main inner cities – London, Birmingham, Manchester or Glasgow – to see people queuing at soup kitchens or begging on the streets to buy food. They are the hard-hitting and visible aspects of food poverty – the tip of a much larger iceberg. There remain elements that we fail to see – for example, parents who go without food in order to feed their children or who are not able to afford healthy choices, but only the cheaper, less nutritious alternatives. This is the reality in twenty-first century Britain.

What is food poverty?

Food poverty can be defined as:

> the inability to acquire or consume an adequate quality or sufficient quantity of food in socially acceptable ways, or the uncertainty that one will be able to do so.[1]

Addressing food poverty is complex and is intrinsically linked with addressing the economic circumstances of poorer families. Families surviving on low incomes face many financial pressures and whilst expenditure on rent, heating bills, council tax and debt or social fund repayments are fixed, the amount spent on food is in the flexible budget category. For many of these families, living day-to-day and looking to save money in order to make ends meet, it is often the food budget that suffers in times of financial difficulty.

Despite recent increases in incomes and state support through tax credits, some parents are still unable to provide healthy food for their family. Today's benefit levels are not sufficient for a family to maintain a healthy diet. This is partly due to an increasing gap in the cost of eating healthy food compared with less healthy alternatives. According to research by NCH children's charity, healthier foods typically cost 15 per cent more than less healthy versions and are not always available – a significant factor that discourages those on a tight budget from making healthy food choices.[2]

Clearly, lack of money has a direct effect on the ability of low-income families to provide a nutritious diet. It has been calculated that low-income families with one adult in employment and two children spend, on average, £50.71 on food each week. This compares with £62.84, the minimum amount required to provide such a family with an adequate diet.[3] This situation has a knock-on effect on dietary and eating patterns within these families.

Some see healthy eating as the responsibility of the individual and failure to eat healthily as a result of irresponsible spending choices. However, research suggests that it is unfair to blame parents and children for the failure to maintain a healthy diet. In fact, in a recent survey of the diets of children and families on low incomes, NCH found that 46 per cent of the low-income parents surveyed had gone without food in the last 12 months in order to provide for their family, and more than a quarter stated that they were not able to give their children the food they would like.[4] That parents were unable to give their children the food they would like, even though they were going without food themselves, reinforces just how bad the situation is.

The same research also highlighted that food consumed by these families was nutritionally poor, with only a minority of children eating vegetables frequently, and more than a quarter never eating vegetables or salad. When comparing these findings to a similar NCH study in 1991 it is clear that there has been very little improvement in the diets of families on low incomes over the last 12 years; a shameful record in itself.[5]

Food security

Removing the financial obstacles alone is not enough to end food poverty. If we are to overcome food poverty we need to address other factors, such as access to food, consumer choice and issues about food security. Dowler, Turner and Dobson provide a definition of food security:

> Food security means that all people at all times should have physical and economic access to sufficient, affordable, safe and nutritious food necessary and appropriate for a healthy life, and the security of knowing that this access is sustainable in the future. In Britain, this means people need:
>
> * access to food – to have enough money and to be able to reach the kind of shops which stock the foods needed for good health at affordable prices;
> * to enjoy choice – the food people can buy has to be both safe, and necessary or appropriate for a healthy life and for the culture in which they live;
> * freedom from fear – as far as possible people should be free from anxiety about whether they will be able to eat properly.[6]

Families living on low incomes experience a number of barriers to accessing healthy foods. For instance, the location of many supermarkets and other major food stores in out-of-town shopping centres has had a negative impact on many low-income families living in inner cities. The ability to buy fresh produce has become a major problem for such families, with the only viable option being that of local shops, limited in choice, low quality and priced at a premium. Compounding this problem, a large percentage of low-income families are reliant on public transport and have to spend a higher proportion of their potential food budget on transport costs compared with more affluent families. This is a situation that also affects many low-income families living in rural areas whose nearest supermarket may be many miles away. NCH has estimated that this can add an extra 23 per cent to the cost of their shopping – a considerable reduction in food purchasing power.[7] Such factors have added to the difficulties that families face in providing a healthy diet.

The importance of healthy eating

You are what you eat; failure to maintain a healthy diet can have many adverse impacts. Women with unhealthy diets are more likely to give birth to underweight babies, and children deprived of necessary nutrients, particularly during their early years, are more likely to suffer from health problems later on in life.

Unhealthy eating increases the chances of suffering from heart disease, high blood pressure, type 2 diabetes, dental problems and certain cancers. Concern recently has been focused on the alarming levels of obesity in Britain – we now have the third highest obesity rate in the world behind the United States and Mexico, with those from low-income households disproportionately represented.[8] One in five adults are considered obese, a figure that has tripled in the last twenty years. Even more alarming is the high level of obesity in children: 8.5 per cent of six-year-olds are obese, increasing to 15 per cent of 15-year-olds.[9] Each year, obesity is claiming thousands of lives. It has been calculated that 34,100 deaths in England in 2002 were attributable to obesity; the overall cost of obesity is between £3.3 and £3.7 billion.[10] This is a figure that will only increase unless serious action is taken to change our diets and lifestyles.

The effects of poor nutrition will follow a person throughout her or his life. It is well documented that a number of disease rates linked to diet are more prevalent in lower socio-economic classes. Elizabeth Dowler, in *Poverty Bites*, identifies that ill-health, such as dental disease, asthma and high cholesterol, is higher among those on low incomes. Furthermore, illnesses that affect adults, such as cancers of the lung and stomach and bone disease are all linked to food that is higher in salt and sodium, and low intakes of vegetables and fruit – food that those on low incomes are more likely to eat.

Medical advances can help us treat some of these diseases, but the best form of cure is prevention: something which starts with healthy eating.

Policy developments

For most of the 1980s and 1990s there was very little discussion about food poverty in Britain. Conservative governments dismissed the notion that food poverty even existed in Britain and, as discussed in Chapter 2, even had for a while a highly visible junior health minister who pointed to irresponsible spending choices as the main reason why poor families were failing to eat healthily. In contrast, under the current Labour government there has been a significant shift in policy thinking, mainly due to its aim of eradicating child poverty and determination to tackle health inequalities. This has led to a number of inquiries and consultations, such as the Acheson inquiry in 1998[11] and the Department of Health's White Paper, *Saving Lives: our healthier nation*, in 1999.[12] In these reports there was an acknowledgment that 'the poorest people often face the highest prices' and of the difficulties people living in deprived and rural areas have in accessing shops with affordable food. However, when we look at the actions of the Government, very little has been done to increase either the accessibility or the affordability of healthy food.

Even in the Government's recent consultation examining the best ways to improve diet and nutrition, the subjects of affordability and accessibility of healthy foods were overlooked.[13] Indeed, the Government's proposed changes to the measurement of child poverty do not include a direct measure of healthy eating.[14]

There are areas, however, in which the Government has taken concrete action to try to improve children's diets, namely schemes such as the Welfare Food scheme and the National School Fruit Scheme in England. But the success of these schemes varies and many initiatives are failing to fulfill their full potential. For example, changes to Healthy Start under the Welfare Food scheme mean that pregnant women and mothers of children in their first year are now entitled to an additional allowance to buy fruit and vegetables, cereal-based foods and milk and formula. While this move is welcome, its impact is limited as the additional allowance is withdrawn after the child's first birthday, even though a highly nutritious diet remains essential for a child's further development.

It is pleasing to see that the Government recognises schools as vehicles to promote healthy eating, but progress in this area has been somewhat disappointing and, in places, contradictory. At the same time as schools are trying to promote the importance of eating fruit through the National School Fruit Scheme, school vending machines selling crisps and chocolate and school equipment being sponsored by companies which sell junk food actively promote the consumption of unhealthy food.

Despite these apparent contradictions, the National School Fruit Scheme seems to be one of the Government's successes, with a majority of parents and children welcoming it and many teachers regarding it as a support to learning about healthy eating.[15] Unfortunately, this cannot be said for some other school-based initiatives.[16] For example, the Healthy Schools initiative, which led to school nutrition action groups and the expansion of breakfast clubs, has shown little evidence of improving children's diets (although there are reports from some schools to the contrary – see Chapter 3). Even where positive moves are made, such as with the introduction of breakfast clubs, schools have to be aware that offering unhealthy foods in place of nutritious ones can have the adverse effect. Research conducted by Sheffield University, for instance, found that children were being offered sausage sandwiches, doughnuts and crisps at some breakfast clubs, and that there was little availability of fruit and cereals. Worryingly, this study also found that those pupils who attended breakfast clubs had exceeded the adult daily salt limit in just this single meal.[17]

Further examination of school meals shows that unhealthy food is not confined to school breakfasts. It has been reported that reductions in school meals budgets have forced school caterers to opt for cheaper options and to provide less healthy meals high in salt, fat and sugar. The pressure to reduce costs in the school meals budget has meant that school lunches are provided for as little as 35p each.[18] It is, therefore, not surprising that in a recent MORI survey nearly half of secondary school pupils believed that school dinners were unhealthy.[19] One would have expected the introduction of minimum nutritional standards for school lunches in 2000, the first standard in nearly twenty years, to have helped address this problem, but in their current form these standards are too general and their impact limited.

What needs to be done?

The importance of maintaining a healthy diet has been recognised by the Government. However, the prospect of healthy eating is beyond the reach of many children in families on low incomes. The high cost of healthy food is a major obstacle for many parents, but it is by no means the only one. Healthy food needs to be accessible as well as affordable. To help achieve this, a coherent package of initiatives is required to remove the various obstacles to healthy eating faced by children from low-income families. It is within this context that schools have an important role to play, providing a vital location in which the Government can ensure healthy eating by children.

By prioritising healthy eating in schools a real difference can be made to the diets of many children and would help tackle the growing health problems that young people face. Healthy school breakfasts (through breakfast clubs) and lunches could significantly increase the nutritious content of a child's diet. However, improving the nutrition of children through schools requires a lot more than offering healthy meals. Today, nearly one in five children entitled to free school meals (330,000 children) fail to take them up[20] and schools need to be more innovative in their approach to school meal provision.[21] The case studies in this book show how this is possible. Not only does the quality of school meals need to improve, but a wider range of related factors need to be addressed. These include the stigma associated with free school meals (something that could be tackled by extending eligibility or providing a universally free service as some local authorities are now doing), ensuring that pupils are effectively involved in deciding school menus, and removing facilities that undermine healthy eating, such as the availability of high fat, salt and sugar products in school vending machines.

We are constantly being warned of the dangers of an unhealthy diet. The costs of not maintaining a healthy diet are borne by everyone, though more intensively by the poorest. The children of today are our country's future; it is socially unjust and economically unwise not to invest in them. Schools are not the only solution to ensuring that all children can eat healthily; adequate incomes are also critical, but they have a vital part to play. They can provide children with the opportunity to eat healthy food and learn about the importance of maintaining a healthy diet. This can only be achieved if government, local authorities and schools all work together and make healthy eating in schools a priority.

Notes

1   E Dowler, S Turner and B Dobson, *Poverty Bites: food, health and poor families*, Child Poverty Action Group, 2001

2   *Going Hungry: the struggle to eat healthily on a low income*, a summary, NCH children's charity, 2004

3   H Parker, *Low Cost but Acceptable: a minimum income standard for working households with children living in Wales*, Family Budget Unit, 2002

4   See note 2

5   See note 2

6   See note 1

7   See note 2

8   *OECD health data 2003*, Organisation for Economic Co-operation and Development, 2003

9   *Tackling Obesity in England*, National Audit Office, 2001

10 House of Commons Health Select Committee, *Obesity*, Third Report of Session 2003/04 Vol I, 2004

11 D Acheson (chair), *Independent Inquiry into Inequalities in Health*, Department of Health, 1998

12 *Saving Lives: our healthier nation*, Department of Health, 1999

13 *Choosing Health? Choosing a Better Diet: consultation on priorities for a food and health action plan*, Department of Health, 2004

14 *Measuring Child Poverty*, Department for Work and Pensions, 2003

15 See *Evaluation Summary: The National School Fruit Scheme*, Department of Health, 2004

16 See note 13

17 'School Breakfast Clubs Serve Junk Food: nutritionists criticise menus of sausage sandwiches, crisps and doughnuts – but no fruit', *Sunday Telegraph*, 14 December 2003

18 'The 35p School Meal and Why We'll Pay Later', *Daily Mail*, 27 May 2004; *Food For Life*, Soil Association, 2003

19 MORI research found 49 per cent of 11 to 15-year-olds believed that school meals could increase problems – for example, poor nutrition and weight gain (http://news.bbc.co.uk/1/hi/education/3353935.stm)

20 P Storey and R Chamberlin, *Improving the Take-up of Free School Meals*, Brief 270, Department for Education and Employment, 2001; analysis of National Statistics, *Statistics of Education: Education and Training Statistics for the United Kingdom*, Department for Education and Skills, 2003, p30, table 2.10

21 See note 18

Two

The role of school meals in tackling child poverty

Ashley Riley

To understand the importance of school meals in the fight against child poverty, why they have received so much criticism and how they can be improved, it is necessary to review their history. The later stages, after 1965, are closely tied to CPAG's own history: in reviewing this, we can shed light on concerns about school meals policy over the last four decades.

School meals, including subsidised school meals, have a long history. Following the introduction of the 1870 Education Act, more and more children from very poor homes began entering schools for the first time. And in **1879**, Manchester became the first city to provide school meals for 'destitute and badly nourished children.'[1]

A parliamentary committee in **1904** reported that the poor physique of volunteers in the Boer War highlighted the problem of under-fed children. It is disturbing that two of the principal reasons we cite today for why school meals are so important – that children will not fully physically develop and may not, as a consequence, be able to fulfil a wholesome and healthy life – were recognised a hundred years ago.[2]

The next fifty years saw a gradual increase in provision of school meals. Over one million children were taking school meals by **1920**, with free milk being introduced four years later. In the early **1940s**, as rationing was implemented across Britain, a national school meals policy was introduced for the first time. Two years after the war in **1947**, with Attlee's Labour Government in place and the post-war welfare state being established, the full cost of school meals in all state schools was met. With the greatly expanded welfare state taking place, the Attlee Government announced the goal of a free midday meal for every school child.[3]

That goal was never achieved and, although the number of children receiving free school meals would almost double over the next 25 years (from 33 per cent in 1944 to 64 per cent in 1972), from its earliest days CPAG campaigned not only against the Labour Government's retrograde action on the service, but also against the stigmatising practices of local education authorities and schools exposed by its branches.[4]

In the early to mid-**1960s** there was growing concern among academics and others that child poverty in Britain was on the increase and that governments were not addressing the issue. The Child Poverty Action Group was founded as a result of that concern. At the same time as CPAG began to lead the anti-poverty lobby, concern grew at the increasing costs of school meals.

In the early **1970s**, the cost of the school meal steadily rose above inflation year on year, from 1s 6d in 1967 to 12p in 1971. Research in **1977** showed that take-up had fallen, but that 61.7 per cent of all school children had a school meal, at a cost of £380 million to the Exchequer.[5]

At the same time, though, the Labour Government received official reports, effectively advocating that school meals be used in an 'overkill' manner to improve the nutrition of children. The Cockerill Committee reasoned that it was not 'safe to assume that all children receive a satisfactory diet at home.'[6] Another committee urged local education authorities and schools, very much in the language of the Education (Provisions of Meals) Act of 1906, to:

> do all they reasonably can [in respect of children] who are inadequately or unsuitably fed at home, and try to ensure that lack of proper nourishment does not prevent them from *taking full advantage of the education provided for them*.[7]

The Wilson Government was being roundly told that, seventy years on, the 1906 argument for school meals remained good and, even if it meant that some children had more nutritious food than they needed, school meals remained a vital tool – as, indeed, they do today. Moreover, governments had, during those seventy years, suggested other reasons for school meals, so that a CPAG report, published in 1980, identified no fewer than 13 *official* arguments.[8]

Even without the time-honoured case for a meal enabling a child to take full advantage of the education provided, there is a case for using school meals to improve child nutrition *per se*. Getting the right food into children is not easy, but as children are compelled to attend school, we have a captive gathering to whom to offer nutritious food, at least five days a week in school terms. Of course, nutritious school meals are of no advantage to children if they are excluded from them. Subsequent chapters of this book illustrate some imaginative ways of bringing children back to the school meal table.

The watershed in the governmental retreat from good-quality school meals was in **1980**, as the incoming Thatcher administration shelved official recommendations on this proven recipe for child health and introduced elements of legislation that undid so much of the post-war improvements in the service.

The recommendations were from a working group, chaired by Sir Douglas Black. As part of its 'anti-poverty strategy' in respect of families and children, the group reiterated the case – on both education *and* health grounds – for nutritious school meals, and advocated that these be free for all. It presciently warned that:

> to leave school children, especially young school children, to make their own free choices of [meal] would be wrong... [This would be] likely to lead to increases in obesity and in dental caries.[9]

A strategy to combat poverty did not appeal to Prime Minister Margaret Thatcher, who said that 'poverty was not just the breeding ground of socialism [but] the deliberately engineered effect of it.'[10] So, having declared the expenditure demands of the Black strategy to be 'quite unrealistic',[11] the Government chose to focus on the individual responsibility for unequal health. Edwina Currie, a Conservative Member of Parliament, dismissed the Black working group's approach:

> I honestly don't think the problem has anything to do with poverty. We have problems... we can tackle by impressing on people the need to look after themselves better.[12]

The 1980 Education Act was, therefore, very much in keeping, in its sections reforming school meals, with the Conservative philosophy of rejecting governmental responsibility and making better health the responsibility of the individual.

The beginning of the decline of the universal system was heralded with sections 22 and 23 of the new Act, which gave local education authorities the power to axe completely the school meals service. The only remaining statutory requirements – which were the most basic – were that local education authorities had to ensure children whose parents got supplementary benefit or family income supplement received access to a free meal and that facilities must be provided for those pupils who brought their own food into school.

In **1981** CPAG began campaigning in earnest with the publication of *Badge of Poverty*. It demonstrated how the attitude and actions of the Government on free school meals had compounded, rather than overcome, the problem of stigma.[13] Furthermore, with the number of children living in poverty increasing during the 1980s, the authors recommended that not only should trade unions, political parties, families and all concerned with children's education demand a universal free school meals service, but also that sections 22 and 23 of the 1980 Act should be repealed.

Those recommendations progressed into a national campaign. CPAG's *Annual Report* in 1983 explained that throughout that year the organisation had been:

> ...involved in calling the attention of local education authorities who were threatening to cut or abolish their school meals service to the evidence that poverty among children would thereby be deepened and extended...[14]

The erosion of the service, however, continued and there were further reductions in the number of children taking both school meals and free school meals. In **1986** a new Social Security Act came onto the statute book. Children whose parents were in receipt of income support were still eligible for free school meals, but those who received family credit had the price of the meal nominally included in the benefit. This major change – giving money rather than providing a meal – led to a large number of children losing their entitlement. In **1987**, only 49.4 per cent of children took school meals – since 1970 there had been, on average, a 1 per cent reduction in school meal take-up every year.[15] At the same time, child poverty continued to increase, exacerbated by the new rules on free school meals.[15] The Government had no anti-poverty agenda to halt this rise.

The long period of Conservative government, for almost two decades, saw child poverty rise from 1 in 10 children living in low-income households in 1979 to 1 in 3 by the middle of the 1990s.[16] In **1991**, twelve years into the Thatcher administration, the introduction of compulsory competitive tendering led to many school meals services being contracted out to the private sector, accompanied by reductions in quality.

CPAG continued to campaign for wider eligibility and its local branches increasingly raised the issue in their local media. Throughout the early 1990s eligibility rules were tightened for income support, which meant that only people working under 16 hours a week were eligible to claim free school meals compared with the previous 24 hours. Eleven per cent of local authorities ceased to provide school meals beyond their statutory requirement. In **1995**, less than half of children (45 per cent) in England took school meals.[17]

CPAG summarised the situation at the time:

> It was, in reality, no longer a national service that could be an effective instrument for government health policy. Over one million poor children were missing out on the right to a free school meal and at least 300,000 did not receive the meal to which they are entitled.[18]

In **1997**, a Labour government was elected to office with a landslide majority and a mandate 'to deliver social justice'.[19] Prime Minister Tony Blair spoke of his intent to deliver to all the country but recognised the particular importance of improving life for the poor: '...if we do not raise the standard of living of the poorest people in Britain we will have failed as a government...'[20]

If Labour needed evidence in its formative years of government that school meals were as important as ever, it came in a number of key reports. The Acheson report on health inequalities (which updated the 1980 *Black* report and the 1986 *Whitehead* report) argued that there was a case for extending provision of free school meals, which would in turn improve the nutrition of the whole family.[21] At the same time, the Department for Education and Employment published *Eating Well*, which reported that for many school children, the school dinner was still the main meal of the day.[22]

An opportunity for CPAG to lobby the incoming government on the importance of school meals arrived in March **1998**. The Chancellor delivered his second Budget, introducing a new system of financial support for those on low incomes – working families' tax credit. At the time, only children whose families were on income support or jobseeker's allowance were entitled to a free school meal. CPAG argued that if a government recognised a family's income as being sufficiently low to need support through working families' tax credit, then surely those families should be entitled to a free school meal.

CPAG's 'Free School Meals for Children who Need Them' campaign was launched with the publication of *Filling the Gap: free school meals, nutrition and poverty* in **1999**. This called for:

- entitlement to free school meals to be extended to all school children whose parents received working families' tax credit or disabled person's tax credit;

- take-up of free school meals to be maximised; *and*
- the introduction of minimum nutritional standards for school meals and the development of nutritional education in schools.

Despite Labour's concern for social justice, these demands were not met at the time.

Throughout the campaign, CPAG was concerned about the large number of children who were entitled to free school meals, but who did not take them. In **2001**, we collaborated with the Department for Education and Employment to commission research considering how the take-up of free school meals could be improved.[23] The subsequent report, published later that year, listed the key factors that inhibited take-up. These included:

- fear of stigma and bullying;
- easily identifiable tokens or free tickets for those entitled to free school meals which fuelled stigma;
- poor quality of food on offer;
- lack of awareness on the part of parents of their entitlement.

The report revealed some shocking cases of schools in which children receiving free school meals sat apart from their friends and in which the free 'tickets' did not cover the cost of a basic meal and children were forced to put back food before they got to the payment till. There were also examples of schools with a high percentage of Muslim pupils, yet pork was often the only food choice available.

In **2001**, the Government introduced new, compulsory national nutritional standards.[24] Despite their aim to '...give children a varied and balanced diet to...help young people improve their concentration and fulfil their potential both inside and outside school' – language redolent of 1906 and 1975 – the new standards only required caterers to provide foods from at least two nutritional groups, such as carbohydrates and dairy products. CPAG has concerns about the adequacy of these standards and the latest research from the Department for Education and Skills has shown that despite the large majority of secondary schools meeting the standards, unhealthy options are still being favoured over healthy food.[25]

In April 2003 child tax credit replaced working families' tax credit. Those families entitled to full child tax credit were entitled to free school meals for their children. This new financial support structure led to an additional 75,000 children across Britain being entitled to a free school meal. CPAG welcomed this, but warned that, while stigma and bad practice went unchecked, thousands of newly entitled children would miss out.

Despite the manifest problems with the school meals service, school meals continue to play a fundamental role in supporting children's education and development. This is, however, less than the protective and enabling role they could – and should – play in the lives of our poorest children. Government statistics in 2003 show that child poverty fell from 4.3 million in 1996/97 to 3.6 million in 2002/03.[26] While the Government has made very encouraging progress on reducing child poverty, the limited household budgets of many low-income families mean that children can go without healthy and nutritious food at home. Many poor children in the UK still require a hot nutritious meal at school and often rely on this as their only meal of the day.

There is growing support for the re-introduction of universal school meals. Tom Watson, the Member of Parliament for West Bromwich East, wrote in *The Guardian* in April this year that the potential benefits of a programme of free school meals are so great that we cannot afford to ignore them.[27] Free school meals for all, both in 1904 and in present-day Britain, would make a major difference to the future physical development of children. CPAG continues to campaign for a universal system in 2004 with the knowledge that an all-inclusive system would eradicate stigma and improve the take-up for those from low-income homes (as it does with child benefit, which has a 98 per cent take-up rate).

David Kidney MP has recently tabled a Bill in the House of Commons on food in schools. This Bill has called on the Government to assist schools in implementing food policy within individual schools.

So there is growing momentum to place school meals higher on the Government's agenda. One hundred years after a parliamentary committee reported on the poor physique of children, the need to legislate to improve school meals is as strong as ever.

The link between nutrition and poverty is fundamental. School meals can, and must, once again play a pivotal role in addressing the inability of low-income families to consume or purchase healthy food. Evidence on nutrition shows the importance of school meals in diets, as well as the benefits of healthier food. The examples in this book show some, often simple and cost-effective, ways in which both the 'offer' can be improved *per se* and take-up of free school meals can be maximised. Much can be done now, and much can be gained by doing so. Our case studies provide us with a guide.

Notes

1 W McMahon and T Marsh, *Filling the Gap: free school meals, nutrition and poverty*, Child Poverty Action Group, 1999

2 E Dowler, S Turner and B Dobson, *Poverty Bites: food, health and poor families*, Child Poverty Action Group, 2001

3 House of Commons *Hansard*, 19 February 1947, col 1311

4 See for example, T Lynes, 'The Dinner Money Problem, *Poverty* 10, Child Poverty Action Group, 1969, pp13-15

5 See note 1

6 Working Party on Nutritional Aspects of School Meals, *Nutrition in Schools*, Her Majesty's Stationery Office, 1975, para 10

7 Department of Education and Science, *Catering in Schools*, Her Majesty's Stationery Office, 1975, para 79 (1906 language in italics: emphasis added)

8 D Bull, *What Price Free Education?*, Child Poverty Action Group, 1980, p25

9 P Townsend and N Davidson (eds), *Inequalities in Health: Black report*, Penguin, 1988

10 M Thatcher, *The Downing Street Years*, HarperCollins, 1993, pp627 and 646

11 See note 9, p31

12 E Currie, *Life Lines: politics and health 1986-1988*, Sidgwick and Jackson, 1989, p12

13 L Bissett and J Cousins, *Badge of Poverty: a new look at the stigma attached to free school meals*, Child Poverty Action Group, 1982

14 *Annual Report*, Child Poverty Action Group, 1983

15 A Walker and C Walker, *The Growing Divide: a social audit 1979-1987*, Child Poverty Action Group, 1987

16 M Howard, A Garnham, G Fimister and J Veit-Wilson, *Poverty: the facts*, 4th edition, Child Poverty Action Group, 2001

17 See note 1

18 See note 1, p10

19 *New Labour, New Life for Britain*, Labour Party General Election Manifesto, 1997

20 *The Independent*, 8 December 1997

21 See note 9

22 Department for Education and Employment, *Eating Well,* The Stationery Office, 1997

23 P Storey and R Chamberlin, *Improving the Take-up of Free School Meals*, Department for Education and Employment, 2001

24 National Nutritional Standards for School Lunches, Department for Education and Skills, http://www.dfes.gov.uk/schoollunches/juniors.shtml

25 Food in Schools – a commitment to healthy choice, Press Notice 2004/0135, Department for Education and Skills, 13 July 2004

26 Department for Work and Pensions, *Household Below Average Income 1994/05-2002/03*, 2004

27 *The Guardian*, 7 April 2004

Part two
Good practice

Three

Community partnerships in the London Borough of Newham

Carrieanne Hurley

Newham is a vibrant, inner-city borough just 25 minutes away from the centre of London and in the heart of east London. It is a young, friendly, cosmopolitan community. The pupils in Newham reflect the intricate tapestry of our multi-ethnic borough and make an invaluable contribution to its richness. More than half of our 240,000 population comes from dozens of minority ethnic communities, with more than 137 languages being spoken in the area. It is this diversity which makes living and working here so fascinating.

Resources, both in terms of finance and new energetic thinking, are being channelled into the borough (still one of the poorest in the UK), which is seeing major regeneration. The area has been revitalised in recent years with ambitious and exciting projects on both a small and large scale. With regeneration has come hope – and a new optimism. Investment on an unparalleled scale is making Newham a place of change and opportunity.

Described below are some of the positive school meals and healthy eating initiatives currently taking place in Newham. Many of these have been set up under the New Deal for Communities and Healthy Futures programmes. All our initiatives stress the importance of working in partnership with the community as a whole, rather than seeing the school in isolation.

The New Deal for Communities is a community-based regeneration programme, funded by the Government to reduce deprivation. Newham has money under this programme over a 10-year period. It includes a health focus on preventing ill-health, improving access to primary care, and providing alternative and complementary resources to improve residents' general health and wellbeing. The health theme group is made up of local residents, project managers/co-ordinators, health and social care professionals and other interested parties.

The Healthy Futures programme is a key part of the Government's drive to improve standards of health and education, and to tackle health inequalities. It has a holistic approach to healthy eating and education in schools to ensure the healthy future of our children. The programme aims to create a healthy ethos within schools, improve the health and self-esteem of the school community, and enable children to make healthier choices and improve their educational achievement.

Breakfast clubs

This initiative provides children in schools in the New Deal for Communities area with a nutritious meal before the start of the school day. Our breakfast clubs also aim to redress some of the imbalances in pupils' diets and thereby contribute to improvements in their educational performance. Children have a choice of various cereals, toast, scrambled eggs, baked beans, fresh fruit, yoghurt, fruit juices as well as instant low-fat hot chocolate in the winter. The service is very well received, with between 20 and 80 pupils attending in some of our schools. Pupils' time-keeping has improved as a result and they also appear to be calmer when going into their lessons. This may be because they have a full stomach, and have had time to chat to their friends at the breakfast club and let off steam before classes begin. Some of our clubs are run by schools themselves and some by catering staff. Even some teachers attend.

Healthy eating workshops

We have carried out healthy eating workshops in all the schools in the New Deal for Communities area to talk to pupils about healthy eating and the importance of a balanced diet.

These have ranged from fruit workshops in primary schools, where we made smoothies, talked about where different fruits come from, different textures and tastes of fruit, and why we should be eating it, to fats and sugar workshops in senior schools, where pupils had a quiz on how many grammes of fat were in popular fast-food products. They were all shocked to learn how much fat they were consuming in an average day. As each item was discussed we showed the amount of fat in each product, which we had previously measured out into small containers. We are presently working on a follow-up programme to reiterate the message and evaluate any changes made to pupils' diets.

Healthier lunches

One of the first priorities of Healthy Futures was to compile a recipe book, which was written in conjunction with Newham Catering Service. This incorporates a lot of traditional school meal dishes, but with less fat, sugar and salt than previously. All recipes are colour coded using the traffic lights concept, with green being the healthiest choice with the lowest fat, amber as moderate fat, and red being the highest in fat and something to eat only in moderation. Newham local education authority is installing new menu boards that use this concept and encourage pupils to make healthy choices. The concept works well, as even the younger pupils can recognise the traffic light colours.

A chef trainer has been employed, originally within the New Deal for Communities area with New Deal for Communities funding, and then with £20,000 of Neighbourhood Renewal funding secured via the Healthy Schools initiative. He visits schools to help cooks get back to the basics of good taste and good nutrition. He has been working in individual schools since 2002 and spends up to four weeks in each individual school. After assessing the school's menu from a nutrition and taste appeal perspective, he works with the cook to come up with new options that will appeal to the children and boost their health. As the chef trainer is so busy across the borough, the New Deal for Communities has employed a second trainer to finish training cooks within its own area. Although Neighbourhood Renewal funding has now come to an end, Newham local education authority has extended the training to ensure that all cooks can have access to this one-to-one training.

Pupils now have school meal options such as chicken and salad pitta breads, cheese or tuna filled tortilla wraps, sweet and sour chicken and vegetables, and lamb curry and rice. Cooks also decorate healthy fruit-based desserts to make them more appealing, encouraging children to choose them.

Up to 60 per cent of the schools in Newham are involved in the National School Fruit Scheme, in which fresh portions of fruit are delivered to children on a daily basis. Trends show that children become accustomed to the taste of fruit through the scheme and tend to take up healthier fruit-based options when making school meal choices at lunchtime.

Some schools employ midday meal supervisors, who stand at the front of the lunchtime queue and encourage children to try new foods and choose a healthy balanced lunch.

Newham local education authority carries out an annual survey of pupils to find out what they have been eating, what they perceive as being healthy food and what kind of meal options they would like to see more of in school. This information is fed back to the catering service, so they can improve the choices on offer. The menus are nutritionally analysed in accordance with both the Government's and the Caroline Walker Trust's (an independent advisory group) guidelines, and colour coded to correspond to the traffic light concept.

However, healthy eating is about more than simply changing a few items on the menu. It is most effective when supported in the classroom, such as with the Grab 5! campaign (see Chapter 9), with teachers who are trained in health and nutrition.

SNAGs

School nutritional action groups (SNAGs) have been set up in many schools in the Newham area, giving pupils a chance to air their views about school meals and contribute to improving them. These groups consist of pupil representatives from each year, school governors, teaching staff and representatives from the catering service.

Cook and eat in schools

Cooking sessions with food technology students in senior schools in the New Deal for Communities area are underway, encouraging them to cook healthier recipes and to adopt a balanced diet as a way of life. Celebrity chef Steven Saunders has also visited some of our primary schools to cook with groups of children of all ages to stimulate their interest in food and cooking. This has been highly successful and as a result many schools have now set up their own cooking clubs.

Cook and eat in the community

During the school holidays we utilised school kitchens in order for parents to learn to cook with their children, as we felt that it was important to carry on the healthy eating message in the home. We found that a lot of parents had not cooked much at home for various different reasons, including a lack of experience, confidence or resources. Various dishes were demonstrated that people then cooked with us. We all sat down together to eat lunch. This allowed people to try out dishes at our expense to see if they, or their children, liked them and also to experience how to cook dishes so that they would feel more confident at home. The children also cooked and even the youngest experienced making various dishes, such as bread, fruit salads, fruit kebabs and healthy pizzas. Parents displayed their talents at cooking food from various countries such as Algeria, Malaysia, Hungary and the Caribbean.

Chef Steven Saunders discusses with parents the meals they are about to cook

One Newham resident said:

> 'It's been the best course I've ever attended. I did not enjoy cooking and the children did not have a good selection of foods. Now I am able to cook interesting healthy meals, and my boys also took part in the sessions.'

Celebrity chef Steven Saunders was present and cooked with us. When asked what he thought of the cook and eat sessions, he said:

> 'It is important for people to know how to cook a nutritional meal including fresh vegetables – we should encourage people to eat healthy and nutritional meals.'

Modern Apprentices

We have made links with Whitbread (who have now registered us as a career centre) to enable our students to apply to Whitbread to join its Modern Apprentice programme. This will give them a job with hands-on experience of being a chef and a place on a day release catering course at NVQ level. There are also places for students who wish to be involved in other areas of the hospitality trade.

Four
Increasing take-up in
South Gloucestershire
Kay Knight

South Gloucestershire (established in 1996 as part of the local government reorganisation) is a small unitary authority, located on the northern
fringes of Bristol, with a population of approximately 250,000. It forms part
of the area formerly known as the County of Avon. School meals are
provided in-house by the Education Department's catering division. The
division employs approximately 500 staff, delivering four million meals a
year to 115 infant, junior, primary, secondary and special schools. Within
the authority, there is a requirement to supply around 600,000 free school
meals each year.

In 1996/97, the local school meals service was floundering. Only 22
per cent of children in South Gloucestershire received a school meal; take-
up of free school meals was 69 per cent (414,000 meals a year). There
was a centralised, single-choice menu, imposed on all primary schools,
with a vegetarian meal provided, primarily, on written request. Catering
staff had become de-skilled as a result of the growth in convenience
foods, in addition to which the lack of investment in skills training had led
to a somewhat demoralised workforce.

A review of the service in 1998 focussed on the need for change –
aspiring to achieve targets based on contributing to a sustainable lifestyle,
general health and wellbeing, and delivering nutritionally balanced menus
that were attractive and appetising and actively sought by all children,
regardless of their ability to pay. Consequently, a new management structure was put in place, directly within the Education Department.

By 2002, we had increasing numbers of children eating school
meals (52 per cent and growing). Take-up of free school meals had risen
to 88 per cent; 114,000 more free school meals were being received.
These results would not have been possible without introducing far-reaching changes and consulting with pupils, parents, governors, headteachers, teaching staff and other agencies.

All change!

Initiating change has been difficult. In relation to staffing, it has been necessary to change the whole focus of skills training, concentrating on the need to provide not only good-quality food, but also an inclusive, caring and customer-focussed environment. From walking the job, we became aware of the need to create a positive ambience, within a safe and friendly environment, to encourage a social change in eating habits and enhance the interaction between all pupils, giving the service 'street credibility'.

We therefore embarked on a marketing initiative, branding the school meals service, enhancing the dining rooms (through redecoration, replacement furniture etc), re-equipping kitchens, and planning fun days

PILNING PRIMARY SCHOOL **MENU – Meal Price £1.30** Yoghurt and Fresh Fruit are available daily (v) = Suitable for Vegetarians	Toast – 10p Fruit Tuck – 15p available at mid morning break Jacket Potatoes & Salad Bar Daily
MON	Chicken curry Battered fish portions Vegetable curry (v) Rice / Mashed potatoes Garden peas / Organic carrots / Salad	Chocolate sponge with chocolate sauce
TUE	Homemade pasties / Sausage rolls Cheese & onion pasties (v) Baked beans / Coleslaw / Tomato & cucumber	Ice cream and fruit
WED	Roast beef, gravy Roast chicken, gravy Cheese & vegetable bake (v) Roast potatoes Fresh organic carrots / Fresh cabbage	Sultana sponge with custard
THU	Ham & tomato pasta bake / Savoury mince Cheese & tomato pasta bake (v) Country diced potatoes / Pasta Sweetcorn	Eccles cake with custard
FRI	Fish fingers Sausages Vegetarian burger (v) Chipped/Jacket potatoes Spaghetti hoops / Baked beans / Salad	Iced bun

Minor alterations to this menu may take place due to circumstances beyond our control.
South Gloucestershire Traded & Support Services

Salads, vegetarian options and organic foods are featured on this school menu

and themed menu events linked to curricular activity and complemented by competitions and free gifts.

Following research and consultation with parents, a change in product purchasing was made, to introduce improved, healthier products, local fresh meat, eggs, chicken and organic fruit and vegetables, and to reduce levels of fats, salts, sugar and additives.

We also set about establishing an intensive training programme, including on nutrition and customer care, with staff to ensure that they could provide a more rounded service, in particular to encourage and integrate a higher take-up of free school meals.

Each kitchen manager now produces a menu exclusive to her/his own school, using the fresh and improved products and consulting with parents and children. The lunchtime menu provided offers a multiple choice of meals, including vegetarian dishes, salad bars and daily availability of fresh fruit, yoghurts and milkshakes. We actively encourage communication between parents and kitchen managers to facilitate all special dietary needs and to ensure that all pupils' requirements are met within the service.

But it has not been an easy road to travel and the shift in culture is still taking place. When we initiated fresh meat and vegetables (particularly broccoli) onto the menus, many pupils (particularly those from low-income families) did not have a palate for such foods and resisted selecting them. In some cases, it appeared that such products were outside of their normal diet. However, the training given to staff on how to approach and encourage children to test and taste different foods was aided by reward schemes (such as 'clear plate' stickers) and students slowly became accustomed to a regular diet of fresh meat and vegetables.

Such have been the inroads into cultural change that many of our cooks have been approached by parents requesting copies of the recipes now being used in the schools.

Avoiding stigma and promoting inclusion

In order to encourage participation by parents, especially in relation to free school meals, we introduced a telephone hotline to deal with all enquiries relating to the service. In particular, we receive calls from parents concerned about how to access the free school meal facility. They often express anxieties as to whether the service will be delivered in a sensitive and non-discriminatory manner. An opportunity is therefore given for us to offer reassurance and support and reduce any feelings of stigma about their current circumstances. Indeed, the non-identification of students entitled to receive free school meals is a major factor that influences their willingness to take up their entitlement.

We have a policy of non-identification of free school meals wherever possible in schools. In primary schools, lunch tickets are not issued to pupils. Cash is paid directly to a school administrator and class teachers record as part of the roll call, which pupils are staying for lunch, with free school meal pupils being included in this procedure. At the point of service, therefore, pupils merely queue at the service point to receive their lunch and there is no differentiation between paying and non-paying pupils.

However, in secondary schools, where a cash cafeteria system is in operation, it is relatively easy for onlookers to identify those students who pay for the meal they have selected and those who do not. With this in mind, the catering service has just piloted its first cashless system in a large secondary school.

The system uses swipe cards, issued to all students, which are credited electronically. Pupils receiving free school meals are given the same card, which is automatically credited with the requisite daily spend allowance. As well as operational benefits that have resulted from the introduction of this system, such as a reduction in queuing time and increased throughput, the average daily number of free school meals served has increased by 55 per cent.

Analysis of data collected in primary schools shows a direct correlation between the increase in the numbers eating paid meals and the increase in take-up of free school meals throughout the district. Upon investigation of how the two related, we identified incidents of free school meal pupils wishing to remain with their friends during the lunch period. When their friends were selecting a school lunch, so too would they. However, when their friends chose to bring a packed lunch from home, pressure was brought to bear on their own families to provide a packed lunch in order to facilitate the child's need to do the same. In order to ensure inclusion for all, the catering service introduced a packed lunch option for both paying and free-school meal pupils. The nutritional standards are maintained and the lunches are offered in popular, fashionable lunch boxes. Children have the option to select a lunchbox for regular use, which is subsequently labelled with their name. Although only a small number of students select this option, its availability ensures an equality of access and a more inclusive service.

It is generally accepted that the school meal is often the primary meal of the day for children receiving free school meals and those from low-income families. For this reason, we have maintained and promoted a hot meal service which, we believe, is not only more appealing and substantial, but encourages the social interaction necessitated through a shared eating experience.

The high prices charged for school meals can create a barrier of access for families on low incomes. With this in mind, we have maintained a realistic selling price over the past five years which has enabled us to create an inclusive and affordable service costing only £1.30 for a hot two course meal. We believe this has influenced the numbers receiving meals and, in itself, has created a more viable business.

In addition, we recognised that, especially in less well-off areas, pupils would often attend school having eaten very little, or nothing at all, since the previous day. As a result, we have introduced 13 breakfast services within schools, specifically targeting areas of need. Whilst there is no funding available for the provision of free breakfasts within schools, we have introduced what we consider to be an affordable breakfast menu (for example, egg on toast at 15p). The service has proved to be immensely successful, especially with pupils getting free school meals, many of whom are now joined by their parents.

We believe that we have created a culture of inclusiveness where all pupils, together with their parents and siblings, can enjoy this social time that also provides a healthy start to the day.

Fruit tuck service

It became apparent that, although fruit was available daily as part of the lunchtime meal, it was rarely selected by pupils, for whom a whole piece of fruit was often unattractive and unmanageable. It was also noticed that pupils receiving free school meals seemed consciously to avoid such selection. When we did offer children fruit, we often found that a single bite would be taken from the fruit before it was discarded. There was a reluctance to eat a whole apple which, in its natural form, did not appear to have any street credibility. We were concerned, then, that the overall consumption of fruit was negligible within schools and sought to address this issue in a positive way.

The introduction of a fruit tuck service, where assorted fruit was chopped or diced and served in cones to pupils at a cost of 10p a portion, has proven to be very successful (with over 300,000 portions served within the last academic year). Once more, the affordable price of fruit tuck has resulted in all pupils being able to use the service.

Our intention with these additional services was to encourage healthier lifestyle choices, improved diets and a sustainable culture change for the future. We are currently working with external agencies providing catering services at pre-school and after-school clubs and nurseries to further these aims.

Community partnerships

Previous studies have shown that the diet of low-income families tends to lean towards fatty meat products, biscuits, sweets and convenience foods, rather than one consisting of fresh meat, vegetables, fruit and homemade dishes. Whilst we feel that we can make inroads into children's nutritional intake at school, the culture of change and education in healthier lifestyles needs to be engendered as part of the lifelong learning process throughout the community.

With the advent of extended schools and the commitment to community partnership, we are currently bidding for European funding, with a view to introducing basic cooking, nutritional awareness and housekeeping skills to adult learners within the community. The experience of breakfast and fruit tuck services has given a clear indication that both children and parents from lower-income families have a strong wish to belong to what they see as the 'norm' and will participate wherever possible if access to such services is made available and affordable. We are aware that (certainly in respect of more affluent families) breakfast and fruit tuck services could sustain a higher selling price. However, the intention was to be inclusive – to provide services at prices that were equally affordable and accessible to all.

Conclusions

We do not feel that there has been any magic formula to our increase in take-up of free school meals, but that an amalgam of changes across the service have all contributed to enhancing the availability, credibility and credence of an enjoyable eating experience, shared in a caring and welcoming environment.

The success of the school meals service within South Gloucestershire has been achieved largely through the co-operation and partnership of all stakeholders. Headteachers and school governors throughout the district have been immensely supportive of service developments. Chief officers and councillors, too, have encouraged and embraced changes that are, ultimately, underpinned by the Council's guiding principles.

Our success to date has convinced us that the school meals service can have a social and cultural impact on the health and wellbeing of all pupils, regardless of their circumstances.

Five
Free school meals in Kingston upon Hull
Mary Glew

Extending free school meals provision

Kingston upon Hull's innovative policy for providing free healthy breakfasts and lunches for all of its primary pupils began as a vision of Labour councillor Colin Inglis and was translated into a pledge in the Labour Group's manifesto in 2003. The manifesto stressed the connection between nutrition and achievement, and that in order to learn children must be well nourished. The Labour Group passionately believed that by introducing a free, healthy, integrated school meal initiative it could help break the vicious cycle of educational underachievement, limited life chances and the poor health in later years that can be linked to poor nutrition in childhood.

Following the local government elections in May 2003 and the Labour Group's return to power, the Executive's first task was to devise ways to deliver this manifesto promise and it was decided that the best way would be to seek government permission to introduce the free healthy meals initiative. This was necessary because the Education Act 1996 requires local education authorities to make a charge for refreshments or meals provided by them, unless the pupil is eligible for free school meals. The Education Act 2002 makes provision for local authorities to request a suspension of the statutory requirements if they wish to introduce innovative measures that will contribute to the raising of educational standards. The Executive was able to persuade government ministers to approve the application because Kingston upon Hull's healthy meals initiative breaks new ground in tackling both health and education standards and was a good example of the Council working collaboratively with the primary care trusts.

The Council was told that the Minister of State was 'very keen' to use the power to innovate in order 'to encourage this type of thinking'.

It helped too that although the policy focuses on Kingston upon Hull's children, it is an outward-looking approach that is typical of a pioneering city and which is in tune with national strategies to encourage healthy lifestyles via Sure Start, breakfast clubs, Positive Health in Schools and the work of health action zones and primary care trusts.

Our permission to use the power to innovate came into force on 31 March 2004 and the next step that was necessary for the launch of the flagship policy was for the Executive's revenue budget to be approved at the March meeting of the Council. This was crucial because it contained a budget allocation that would enable the pledge to provide free school meals to be met. Persuading Kingston upon Hull's opposition councillors to support the revenue budget proved impossible and voting at the first of the two Council meetings that were held in March 2004 resulted in a stalemate. At the second meeting voting again resulted in a stalemate and it was only after the votes of two opposition councillors and the casting vote of the Lord Mayor that implementation of the free school meals policy could finally be put into action. Although the original intention was to have a city-wide roll-out of the scheme in three stages, the Executive agreed to a pilot scheme in April 2004 that initially involved eight primary schools and which has now, at the time of writing, increased to fifteen.

Debate continues with some members arguing that the cost of providing free school meals in the pilot schools will lead to cuts elsewhere. The Council's leader, Colin Inglis, has been adamant that this will not be the case. Given that Kingston upon Hull has the highest concentration of type 2 diabetes in the UK, a condition that is linked to poor diet and lack of exercise and which is seen as a key indicator of obesity, itself a national problem, the Executive was determined to steer the policy forward. It believed that by not taking decisive action to tackle health inequalities and raise children's achievements it would be failing in its moral and social duty and its responsibility as a 'corporate parent'. And, as research findings have shown, there is a clear correlation between a healthy diet and improved school performance, attainment, sociability, self-esteem and behaviour, and in the case of breakfast clubs, better attendance and punctuality. Executive members passionately believe that the cost of free breakfasts, fruit, refreshments and lunches, just a fraction of the Council's annual budget, is a very small price to pay for a far-reaching and long-term investment in the health of the city's children and in future generations. We will evaluate how well the scheme is doing, and a number of issues, such as children's attendance, punctuality, behaviour, physical development and educational attainment, will need to be measured over a period of time.

Figure 5.1

Eight Pilot Schools – Free lunches

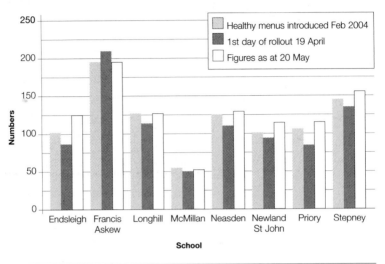

Although the Council's policy is designed to tackle local challenges it has attracted national and international interest from other politicians who wish to introduce similar initiatives or legislation that will allow them to extend the provision of free school meals. Members of the Welsh Assembly have visited Kingston upon Hull to look at the practical issues involved in the delivery of free healthy breakfasts and two MPs, one from the Scottish Parliament, are hoping that Kingston upon Hull's example will add weight to their Private Member's Bills and, at the very least, prompt ministers to take tougher action to ensure children's long-term health and achievements. There has also been keen interest from further afield, with NHK Television in Japan asking for information about our school meals policy and congratulations from a Texas senator who is introducing a free school meals Bill in the autumn. News of our healthy eating policy has spread rapidly and because we care about all children, no matter where they live, we hope that other cities and countries will follow our example, and we are always pleased to help by sharing our experiences.

Healthy school meals

For one in four children, the school meal is the only hot meal they receive each day.[1] It is vital that it is nutritious and well balanced. Indeed, for all children, regardless of their family circumstances, the links between diet and good health must be not only acknowledged but also acted upon. For these reasons, Kingston upon Hull's battle to tackle health inequalities began in February 2004 when the Council introduced a healthy menu, replacing traditional school meals with tasty menus containing reduced levels of salt, sugar and saturated fats and which encourage children to eat more fruit and vegetables. Again, Kingston upon Hull's initiative supports the Government's Healthy Eating Blueprint that aims to tackle the disturbing rise in obesity in children. Healthier cooking methods, such as oven baking and dry roasting, have reduced children's calorie intake by over a third while fat and salt consumption are down by 52 per cent and 70 per cent respectively.

Apart from tackling obesity, a healthy diet can increase longevity and tackle the inequalities that range across cities and the country as a whole. For example, the Council finds it unacceptable that a man living in Kingston upon Thames is likely to live six years longer than a man in Kingston upon Hull. By acknowledging and acting on the link between poverty, diet and health the Council is determined to give Kingston upon Hull's children the best possible start in life, and by beginning the battle in schools, it aims to develop children's understanding of food, nutrition and healthy lifestyles, an understanding that will improve their own life chances and those of their children. It is also hoped that children's increased familiarity with healthy eating will have a knock-on effect on their families.

Children do have strong opinions about the food that they like; they are also influenced by what they are given to eat at home and are subject to peer pressure and advertising by fashionable fast food outlets. The Council was hardly surprised to find that the consumption of the healthy meals in the first weeks of the scheme suffered a temporary 'blip'. Understandably, some parents were concerned that their children would not eat the healthy food and would go hungry; some were convinced that a healthy lunch would consist of only a glass of milk and prunes or other bizarre options and one anxious parent rang her daughter's primary school after being told by her child that she had eaten a pudding that contained prawns! Needless to say the headteacher was able to reassure the parent that it was actually prunes.

Although amusing, this story does illustrate the lack of understanding about healthy eating and the need to communicate effectively with everyone involved in, or affected by, the practical delivery of the policy: teachers, school staff, school governors, parents and children. For this reason the healthy meals policy was launched at the 'Eat Well, Do Well' conference in March 2004. This was very well attended by headteachers, teachers, governors, teachers' aides, local education authority officers and advisers, primary care trust representatives and officers from a range of Council directorates. The conference gave delegates the opportunity to listen to health and education professionals, gain practical guidance on the implementation of the policy, and take part in discussions and question and answer sessions. Stephen Twigg MP, Parliamentary Under Secretary of State for Schools, spoke at the conference via a satellite link from Westminster and delegates were also able to put questions to him.

To ensure that the message about the importance of healthy eating continues to spread, six area catering supervisors from Kingston upon Hull have been visiting schools to spread the word, and Kingston upon Hull catering staff are responding personally to any letters or telephone calls from parents. Schools have sent sample menus to parents, teaching staff are leading by example and joining children at lunchtime to eat the same meals and midday supervisors and school cooks are encouraging children to try the new healthy menu. Catering staff are listening to what children have to say about the new menus and, where necessary, the menus are being amended. This approach acknowledges that children have rights and choices and is one sure way to ensure that children not only eat their meals, but that they also enjoy them.

To help develop children's understanding of the importance of healthy eating and to help convince them that healthy meals can be just as enjoyable as burgers and chips, we planned a number of events at which primary children could learn more about food, diet and the importance of exercise. For the first event, held in May 2004, the owner of a local Michelin star restaurant very generously donated the services of four of his chefs to take part in cookery workshops with children from three primary schools. This was a great success and we aim to repeat it. Watched by their parents, the children learned how to make smoothies for breakfast, salads and omelettes for lunch and even how to fillet fish for dinner. The event was an excellent mix of learning, tasting and fun, and included lunch for the children, their teachers and parents with the Lord Mayor, Councillor Ken Branson.

We know that this approach is working and that numbers are increasing. For any local authority planning to follow suit, our advice would be: to not get put off by the first hurdle or criticism; to stand by your conviction; and to make sure that members, chief officers and everyone that is involved supports and drives the programme. This has certainly been the case in Kingston upon Hull where chief officers have, through their direct involvement, enthused others with their passion and determination to make this scheme a success.

Breakfast clubs

The decision to introduce universal, free, healthy breakfast clubs in primary schools was based on the fact that a number of breakfast clubs in the city, funded through the Children's Fund, would cease when the funding dried up. Secondly, the research from both the local education action zone and the education action zone policy showed that they had made an impact upon children's achievement and attendance. The Council did not want to see the excellent work that has been carried out in some of Kingston upon Hull's schools grind to a halt. Despite the fact that breakfast is an important meal, it is estimated that 6 per cent of all children aged 6-18 miss breakfast, many because their parents do not have the time to prepare it or because of economic factors. That children should miss one of their daily meals and their healthy growth and development suffer as a consequence is not acceptable in Kingston upon Hull.

The importance of a healthy breakfast for children has long been recognised by health and education experts and the balanced meal provided by breakfast clubs meets many of children's needs and addresses many of the problems experienced by schools. There is a wealth of research evidence to show that children who attend breakfast clubs begin the school day on time, feeling well nourished, settled, alert and ready to learn.[2] They will also have been cared for in a safe, supervised and relaxing environment that meets the childcare needs of working parents. Breakfast clubs give children the opportunity to socialise with other children from different age groups and help to address some of the problems, such as bullying, which can stem from some children's poor social skills. Discussions with headteachers and teaching and catering staff in Kingston upon Hull schools have shown that the 29 breakfast clubs (22 initially, with five more launched on 27 June 2004) are beginning to deliver all that was hoped for and more. A number of headteachers have told us that teachers are reporting improved pupil attendance and the fact that children are more alert in the morning. One headteacher has also described how the breakfast club has become an integral part of her school's education programme: a time in which children enjoy their food in an unhurried atmosphere, have discussions and learn. Pupil wellbeing has become inextricably linked with whole school wellbeing and breakfast clubs are part of 'opening up that whole box of what it is that children need besides good teaching and in addition to the effective use of resources in the raising (school) standards agenda' (Janet Adamson,

Attendance at breakfast clubs

Breakfast clubs	19 April 2004	28 May 2004
	First day intro FSM pilots	
Adelaide	30	54
Bethune	0	20
Clifton	9	15
Coleford	20	36
Collingwood	51	50
Dales	35	42
Dorchester	41	0
Estcourt	25	79
Fifth Avenue	25	45
Maybury	28	60
Midmere	0	38
Mountbatten	0	54
Newland Avenue	26	46
Oldfleet	28	31
The Parks	21	33
St Charles	28	23
St James	24	27
St Richard's	42	49
Sidmouth	38	32
Southcoates	12	24
Thorpepark	19	0
Wansbeck	28	53

Headteacher, Clifton Primary School). It is also part of the bigger agenda for developing extended schools in Kingston upon Hull.

Attendance at the breakfast clubs is being closely monitored and the figures are exceptionally encouraging, with some clubs more than doubling or trebling attendance. We are already seeing the immediate benefits and confidently look forward to those that will produce long-term gains in the health and life chances of our children and their children too.

Free school lunches

Since 19 April 2004 free school lunches have been available to all children at 15 of Kingston upon Hull's primary schools and, as a result of the Labour group retaining control of the council in the local government elections in June, this will be expanded across the city. This pioneering initiative, introduced to eradicate child poverty and the social stigma attached to the current free school meals system, is the first of its kind to be introduced by a local authority. It has been pioneered because we know that across the UK over 330,000 children currently eligible for free school meals do not take up their entitlement.[3] Sometimes this is because of their parental perception of the stigma that is associated with free school meals, drawn perhaps upon their own experiences or memories. Very often it is also because of children's fear of standing out, of being socially isolated, or of being teased or bullied by other children. Many parents are also unaware of their entitlement, of how the system works and how they can apply.

Equally disturbing is the fact that many children live in poverty and yet they are not entitled to free school meals. For many of their parents, the cost of school meals may not be affordable, but by providing a universal benefit Kingston upon Hull is ensuring that there is the potential for everyone to take up the offer of a free school meal and there should be no risk of any child slipping through the net. The Council Executive always knew that by biting the bullet it would invite criticism from opposing political parties and from a small section of the general public. The Labour Group has been accused of insulting the many caring and loving parents who ensure that their children are well nourished, of subsidising parents on good incomes and even of depriving children of their daily choice of burgers and chips. Its response has been to stand firmly by the pledge made in 2003 to improve the health, diet and educational attainment of *all* of Kingston upon Hull's children, regardless of their family circumstances. Its vision is summed up in four simple words: Eat Well, Do Well; a vision that is already being transformed into a bigger and brighter picture.

Notes

1   CPAG Free School Meals campaign, www.cpag,org.uk
2   C Street and P Kenway, *Food for Thought: breakfast clubs and their challenges*, New Policy Institute, 1999
3   Free School Meals: are you missing out?, www.raisingkids.co.uk/ac/edu_06.ASP

Six

Rebranding: Glasgow's Fuel Zone

David Parry

Fuel Zone

Background

Direct and Care Services is the service department of Glasgow City Council responsible for providing eight major services, including school catering, to the residents of the city. Glasgow's 197 primary schools and 29 secondary schools have 80,000 pupils to feed on a daily basis. We have been able, using a holistic approach to healthy eating, to develop an ethos that promotes choice for pupils, while simultaneously educating and motivating them to select healthier options. This has been achieved through the introduction of Fuel Zone and also through other initiatives, such as Fruit Plus, Glasgow's Big Breakfast and Glasgow's Refresh.

In 1996 a detailed review of the existing secondary school meals service was carried out. It had become evident that the school children of the city had very negative perceptions of the service, which was largely under-subscribed. Furthermore, there were real concerns about the general state of the health of Glasgow citizens. With research having highlighted the importance of targeting audiences at a young age in a bid to improve eating habits, Direct and Care Services was tasked with the job of developing a business strategy aimed at tackling these challenges.

As a result, the strategic decision was taken to re-vamp completely the existing school meals service in secondary schools and trade under a whole new branding concept known as 'Fuel Zone'. Although the brand varies slightly between primary and secondary schools, it has gone a considerable way toward improving perceptions and exposure to the principles of healthy eating and healthy lifestyles.

Effective marketing planning and strategy development provided the framework for the successful growth of the Fuel Zone brand.

Objectives

The objectives of the project were:

- to improve the use of the school meal service by 50 per cent over a five-year period;
- to increase the take-up of free school meals by 35 per cent over the same period of time;
- to improve perceptions of the school meal service, thus raising its profile and image;
- to have a positive influence on healthy eating choices; *and*
- to reduce take-up of unhealthy food items, such as chips, by 40 per cent over five years.

Market research

Market research was considered by the Direct and Care Services management team to be a critical element of the business planning process to develop a newly branded, up-beat modern service. The team was determined to shift from a previously inward-thinking focus towards an outward, customer/marketing orientation.

Employing a stratified random sampling technique based on gender, age and school attended, extensive consultation consisting of questionnaires, focus groups and discussion forums was carried out with pupils, teachers and parents. The purpose of this research was to identify the factors that would encourage children to use the school meals service rather than an alternative, and hence shape the direction and focus of the business strategy. The sample of children involved in the research came from a wide range of socio-economic backgrounds, representative of the general school population throughout the city.

The initial market research identified that:

- only 32 per cent of pupils ate school meals;
- of those entitled to free school meals, a mere 45 per cent made use of the service;

- children held negative perceptions of the service environment, such as slow and institutionalised service in drab dining halls;
- 80 per cent of pupils ate chips on a daily basis;
- healthy options comprised only 30 per cent of the school meal menu; *and*
- generally, school meals had no 'street cred'.

Such findings highlighted the need for drastic measures, both from an operational and commercial viewpoint. In a commercial sense, it was evident that a re-vamp of school meals was necessary to lift the profile of the service and encourage pupils back into the dining hall. However, more fundamental, serious forces, such as the city's poor dietary habits and lack of exposure to healthy eating regimes, were at play and in desperate need of being addressed.

Given the fact that our 'customers' were children, achieving the correct balance between freedom to choose and ensuring the chosen food was healthy was critical to the outcome of the project. It was thought that if healthier options were simply imposed and pupils were not at liberty to make their own decisions concerning dietary choices, they would simply 'vote with their feet', discounting the school meal service as a potential alternative to high street shops. Although this would result in perhaps a better diet of those who used the service, the outcome would ultimately be lower usage, high wastage and little or no opportunity to influence diet.

Marketing strategy

Phase one: April 1996

In light of the research findings, it was evident that a strategy to entice pupils back into the dining hall, while simultaneously improving their overall dietary habits, was essential. A choice-promoting approach was adopted, giving children the freedom to take the food items of their preference. This was based upon the rationale that greater potential existed to encourage pupils into the dining hall where it was considered easier to educate, motivate and promote healthier eating.

Following on from the research, a multi-phase strategy was developed and implemented. The first phase focussed primarily on drawing pupils back to the table. Throughout this phase the modernised branded service, Fuel Zone, was introduced.

With limited budgets to achieve the radical turnaround required across all 29 secondary schools, external funding was the only option. Major international players in the food and drink industry agreed to fund the refurbishment of six schools each. The refurbishment programme was successful in modernising the appearance of the dining hall. New service styles modelled on those used by high street giants like McDonalds and KFC were implemented. The focus of the new service was bright, colourful, fast and heavily branded. Menus were also modelled on what would be available to the students on the high street, including pizzas, burgers, hot dogs, sandwiches and salads. This was successful in improving pupils' perceptions of school meals and was a huge contributor in attracting them to eat within the school. The revenue generated from the sponsored refurbishments was sufficient to cover the cost of rolling out the scheme across the remaining 17 schools.

Students choosing their meals from the new-style Fuel Zone

Phase two: April 2000

In phase two of the strategy, having won the battle of recapturing the patronage of pupils, the priority was to influence dietary habits. Our research in Glasgow had indicated that:

• 69 per cent of pupils had school meals;
• 68 per cent of free meals were taken;

- pupils perceived the service to have a modern image and be fast;
- 70 per cent of pupils took chips;
- there was a heavy emphasis on branded products; *and*
- 45 per cent of the menu comprised healthier options.

It was evident that after only three years we had already achieved the initial objective of improving take-up of the school meals. The remaining challenge was therefore to influence choice in favour of healthy options. This led to a radical campaign that involved the following changes:

- a new menu range with greater emphasis on healthy foods, such as baked potatoes, pasta and rice-based salads;
- improved partnership working with NHS Greater Glasgow;
- complete re-branding. All menu boards, tray slides, food packaging and labels carried the Fuel Zone brand with reference to sponsors and suppliers entirely removed;
- tariff incentives with special price promotions for healthy items;
- a cashless catering system to eliminate the stigma of free meals and therefore improve take-up; *and*
- ongoing consultation carried out with pupils.

Secondary Fuel Zone Menu Sample

To support the brand development a marketing team was established, with representatives from operations, IT and marketing. Fuel Zone was promoted by:

- innovative sales promotions incorporating the use of scratch cards linked to the sale of healthy foods, offering pupils the opportunity to win tickets to see the latest bands in concert and films at the cinema;
- a publicity campaign that included visits to schools with the high profile music group, The Honeyz;
- newsletters about the service and healthy eating targeted at both pupils and parents;
- a website (www.fuelzone.co.uk); *and*
- a city-wide healthy eating points award competition each term.

Phase three: April 2004

Phase three of the Fuel Zone strategy is the current stage which involves the integration of the existing points award programme in the cashless catering system with the Fuel Zone website. Points are gathered when students purchase healthy meals, can be collected over time and can be exchanged for goods/prizes of the pupil's choice from an online prize catalogue. It is considered that this will not only provide a long-term incentive for pupils to use the Fuel Zone service and eat healthily but will also provide yet another vehicle for measuring and monitoring the scheme.

How successful have we been?

Comments from pupils in September 2003

	Excellent	Good	Satisfactory	Poor	Total
Service quality	206	145	102	47	500
Menu range	166	198	78	58	500
Décor	74	222	147	57	500
Food quality	101	236	111	52	500

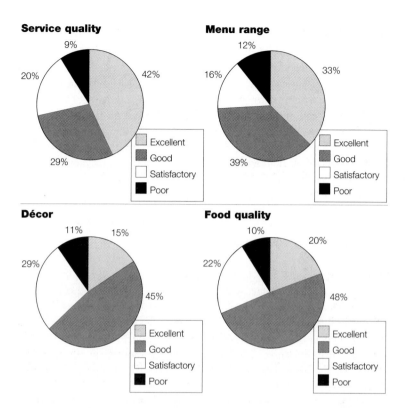

Service quality

- Excellent 42%
- Good 29%
- Satisfactory 20%
- Poor 9%

Menu range

- Excellent 33%
- Good 39%
- Satisfactory 16%
- Poor 12%

Décor

- Excellent 15%
- Good 45%
- Satisfactory 29%
- Poor 11%

Food quality

- Excellent 20%
- Good 48%
- Satisfactory 22%
- Poor 10%

Performance indicator	Pre-Fuel Zone	Fuel Zone (2000)	Fuel Zone (2003)
School meal take-up	32%	69%	74%
Free meal take-up	45%	68%	71%
Healthy food intake	39%	50%	68%
Healthier options on menu range	30%	45%	50%

The Fuel Zone initiative has now been in operation for seven years. Pupils' perceptions of the school meal service and satisfaction have improved significantly. Furthermore, children are far more responsive to the healthy eating message. With current competitive forces from the commercial market and considerable political restraints, this is a considerable achievement. The service has also achieved a full cultural transformation from a previously inward-focussed service to a much more customer-centric approach to business.

Fruit Plus

The Fruit Plus initiative was launched in Glasgow's pre-5 and primary schools in 2001. It involves the provision of free fruit to all pupils in the classroom on a daily basis. As part of this project special teaching packs that integrate the principles of healthy eating into the school curriculum have been developed to help educate and motivate pupils toward healthier food choices. Initially, this project involved providing fruit on three days in the school week, but due to its success and popular demand this has been extended to five days.

Glasgow's Big Breakfast

This flagship service was first introduced to schools across the city in 2002. It is a £1 million initiative that allows all 40,000 primary school pupils in Glasgow access to a free, nutritious breakfast prior to the start of the school day. Rationale for the project comes from the well-documented fact that eating breakfast can increase concentration levels and encourage school attendance, thus increasing attainment levels. It presents pupils with the opportunity to meet with friends, under supervision and in a safe environment prior to the start of their school day. The menu has recently been given a significant boost with a choice of cereals, porridge, beans on toast, and unlimited items such as fruit, yoghurt and cheese are now available. A variety of promotional techniques has been introduced to encourage awareness of, and attendance at, the service and take-up has reached as high as 58 per cent in some schools.

Glasgow's Refresh

This project was introduced across all Glasgow primary and secondary schools in 2003 following research demonstrating the benefits of drinking water in relation to physical and academic achievement. The £1.5 million initiative has witnessed the installation of mains-fed water coolers in every school and the provision of free sports water bottles to all 80,000 pupils in the city. Promotional materials have included information leaflets and bookmarks, which communicate the importance and benefits of drinking water.

Pick 'n' mix

As part of the primary school meal service, a pick'n'mix bar is available to all pupils who take a school lunch. This allows pupils to select as many items as they wish from a variety of healthy options including fruit and vegetable, soup, milk, bread and yoghurts to complement their main meal choice. There is no additional cost and it is fully available to all pupils taking school meals. Since its introduction in 2003, there has been an increase in take-up of such items by most pupils, achieved through effective and high-profile presentation, display options and user-friendly packaging. The core benefit of this initiative is that the emphasis on, and availability of, healthy choices satisfies all appetites. A further addition, introduced in April 2004, is that free milk is available to all pupils in every primary school across the city at lunch time, regardless of whether they take a school meal or not.

Future initiatives

Although Direct and Care Services has been successful in revolutionising the catering services in Glasgow schools, we recognise that further improvements are required. The following areas represent scope for development:

- implementation of the recommendations of the *Hungry for Success: a whole school approach to school meals in Scotland* report by the Scottish Executive (see Chapter 8);
- integration of the existing Fuel Zone website with the cashless catering points award system to create an online loyalty reward programme that will recognise and encourage healthy eating;
- partnership working with the Glasgow Young Scot Card organisation and other public bodies to develop a positive lifestyle card for young people in Glasgow.

Seven

Iris recognition at the Venerable Bede Church of England (Aided) Secondary School, Sunderland

Ed Yeates

The Venerable Bede Church of England (Aided) Secondary School is a new school, built in response to an ever-changing population demographic in south Sunderland, Tyne and Wear. The school is a joint venture between the city of Sunderland local education authority and the Anglican Diocese of Durham. Although the school works in partnership with the city, it is a voluntary aided school and cherishes its right to make decisions about which technologies it will choose to embrace and which it will reject. The school is a greenfield new construction with a phased increase in student numbers over a five-year period. The new building opened to staff and students from Year 7 and Year 8 in September 2003. As a new building, the school sought from its inception to embrace the most modern technologies in its quest to become 'a school for the future'.

The two wards served by the school (Ryhope and New Silksworth) are in the bottom 20 per cent (the most deprived) of all wards nationally using the Index of Multiple Deprivation. Approximately 14 per cent of school children are in receipt of free school meals, but we were aware that more were eligible. There are vast numbers of young people who refuse to take up their eligibility because of stigma or the poor experience of their parents.

A cashless system

Being able to identify those children who take free school meals has been a problem for a number of years and is one that continues in many schools today. Some children getting free meals, for example, have to eat earlier or sit apart from their friends; others have to use free school meal tokens.[1] It is no surprise that where this happens, children may feel stigmatised and may decide not to have their free meal in the future.

In response, the school embarked on a journey of discovery. What systems could we use that would remove the stigma of free school meals and encourage students to take up their entitlement? The local authority's catering service (City Contracting Services) was consulted and a range of options, including swipe cards, was considered. Although swipe cards are useful in a 'cashless' system there are issues concerning their longevity and costs, as typical replacement costs (card cost and operator cost) can result in students who lose their cards failing to replace them. Through City Contracting Services contact was made with CRB Solutions, a small innovative company based in Edinburgh and considered by many to be the market leaders in 'cashless systems'. A number of options were discussed, each with merits and areas of concern.

When considering a cashless catering solution the following key benefits need to be addressed. The system should:

- alleviate stigma associated with free school meals;
- speed up transactions at the till points;
- shorten queues throughout the dining area;
- help to reduce bullying by removing cash from the playground;
- ensure that students remain on-site during lunch breaks;
- increase take-up of school meals (in most cases by 20 per cent);
- facilitate healthy eating campaigns by allowing reward incentives to be promoted by school and catering suppliers; *and*
- automate all back office functions, including the collation, storage and reporting of all data.

The main cashless options are:

- **Swipe cards**. These are considered to be the best option by many, but they are problematic in many ways. The cards are expensive to commission both in card cost and operator time. The cards wear out and the associated costs must be factored into the business plan, and finally, if a student loses her/his card s/he is responsible for buying a replacement. There is some anecdotal evidence suggesting that students in receipt of free meals are unable or unwilling to purchase a replacement card and forego their entitlement until the next card is issued.

- **Thumbprints.** The technology currently exists for this and is used in some primary schools for library purposes. The cost is comparable to swipe cards, but students need to be re-identified every two years as their thumbprints change as they grow. There are also a number of concerns about disease transmission, and health and safety risks. Last, but by no means least, are the associations made between thumbprints and criminality. On balance, it is our view that the negative aspects of using thumbprint recognition outweigh its benefits.
- **Iris recognition.** This technology is currently available as a high security solution for restricted areas. Valued by both the military and airport authorities it provides a safe, fast and cost-effective solution. Each person's iris is unique and through a series of measurements it is possible to identify an individual (even a twin) from others. Like all biometric measures, the concept is simple. We can be identified by our uniqueness and so our data can be recalled from a database. At The Venerable Bede Church of England (Aided) Secondary School we have simply taken the latest technology and made it work for us. The iris recognition system has all of the functionality of a swipe card but is, in the long term, a more cost-effective solution, the financial gains being in part due to the speed at which each transaction is processed. Student details are stored centrally and free meal entitlement is automatically credited to a student's account each day. If a student does not register for school then that day's allowance is removed from the account. By having a number of 'top up' stations around the school it is possible to avoid anyone noticing that a student does not visit a 'top up' station. The main advantages of iris recognition are:

- students only need register once;
- registration lasts for five to seven years – a life-long registration is possible;
- the scanner has no moving parts and should never wear out;
- students have to engage with the system;
- linked to the latest 'Hero' till system, it is fast – approximately 12 transactions a minute;
- it is fun – students enjoy using the technology.

The technical strengths of iris recognition include:[2]

- proven high accuracy – iris recognition has had no false matches in over two million cross-comparisons;

- Iriscode® data bases have the ability to handle very large populations at high speed;
- convenience – all a student needs to do is look into a camera for a few seconds; a video image is taken which is non-invasive and inherently safe;
- the iris itself is stable throughout a person's life, as its physical characteristics do not change with age;
- extremely low maintenance costs.

Costs

The following costings are meant to be indicative only; where schools lack the basic infrastructure there would be an additional resource implication. For many schools, their current tills may prove to be adequate and so the cost would be reduced. In our school we have extended the use of the iris recognition system to incorporate the learning resource centre and potentially access to school outside of the core learning sessions.

5 Iris Scanners	£15,740
1 Enrolment station	£ 1,000
Impact cashless system	£10,340
Database (1,200 students)	£15,000 (this is a multi-application and suits the needs of the school)

Having determined that iris recognition was our favoured option, it was necessary to begin the process of consultation with governors, staff, parents and, most importantly, our students. When news of our use of iris recognition became public we were subjected to a frenzy of media interest. A range of headlines including 'Big Mother' were used to mis-report the product and confuse it with the more invasive retinal scanning technology. Once the actual iris recognition scanners were available in the UK, thoroughly tested and approved, students and parents were able to come and use the technology. The school, now fully conversant with all of the advantages of the system and with the questions posed by civil liberties groups, was able to launch the system to the press. Using our students to explain how iris recognition works, we were able to share our system with others. The feedback was quite the reverse from earlier on and the clear advantages of iris recognition countered the negatives experienced when the technology was first announced.

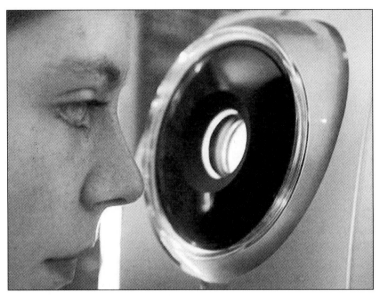

Students' eyes are scanned within a few seconds and their meal account is adjusted accordingly

An improved dining experience

Introducing the iris recognition system was not our only response to the need to improve the quality of school meals within the school. The battle to overcome poor nutrition in students will not be won simply by removing the stigma associated with free meals. We need to have a number of strategies to encourage students not only to take up their entitlement, but to also start making healthy choices.

Even though we are a new school, we were unable to fund a dedicated dining facility. Our school kitchen is quite small, but we hope, through careful design, we have been able to make it a resource that will deliver high quality meals at an acceptable price. Some of our innovations have been taken directly from the private sector and have underpinned our philosophy that the dining experience is of equal importance to the rest of the school day.

Working with our food group (a group of students with an interest in school meals), the school and our catering team have agreed some key features of our dining experience. These include a preference for tables seating four to six, napkins on each table and replacing salt and pepper sachets with pots. The school has also been able to source a fully mobile salad bar, which needs no electricity to run. The food storage containers are placed in a freezer overnight and the freshly prepared food is placed in the containers, which keep the food chilled for up to eight hours. The salad bar can be filled in the kitchen area and then placed anywhere in the school to provide an alternative point of sale or a free sample/trial area for fresh fruit and salads.

As a school we are just starting our journey to ensure that all children have access to healthy food at an affordable price. We have made partnerships with a number of companies. Working together with our local education authority and 'challenging' its current practice, the Secondary Head Teacher Partnership was able to initiate radical changes in the services offered. These included re-branding the City Contracting Services to One Call®, a more responsive and proactive provider of catering solutions. A direct service level agreement with One Call®, including profit sharing, has enabled our school to negotiate its own branded solution. Bede's Bistro will provide high-quality meals for students and staff throughout the day. It will also provide catering for external events, including conferences and fundraisers. Like all schools, we need to ensure a funding stream to re-invest in our facilities. As part of its commitment to our healthy eating strategy, OneCall® sponsored a free fruit and salad bar when the Bistro opened in October 2003.

The need to change the school dining experience of young people is not just a 'nice' thing to do. Research has shown that if our children do not have access to a balanced diet, including complex carbohydrates and fresh fruit and vegetables, their education is affected. Many secondary schools report a peak in poor behaviour before lunchtime as many students are literally working on the energy provided from tea the night before. Through a flexible cashless system we hope to provide access to breakfasts, snacks at break time as well as lunches. We know that for some children it is more appropriate for them to eat at break time as they use their lunch times to play sport or attend clubs. Iris recognition backed by the database should allow all students to access their entitlement to a free meal as and when they want to. By providing a full range of healthy foods, as well as the more traditional 'stodge' which can be made healthier, we hope to encourage our students to eat for their health.

At this book goes to press, we are almost ready to commission our new kitchen. Staff are hard at work unpacking the latest additions to our dining experience – brightly coloured plates that look like porcelain, but are made of melamine. Durable and 'unbreakable' with a four-year guarantee, these fit perfectly on our anti-slip trays (as used on aircraft) to ensure that small children can be confident in collecting and choosing their meals. The signage is bright and incorporates pictures of our youngster in lessons or playing games and advocates a healthy eating message.

Students are all registered on our database with the Iriscode® software. Only time will tell whether we will increase the take-up of free school meals. We must also wait to see if our healthy eating strategy will be effective. Perhaps a once a week ban on chips will eventually be met not with cries of 'oh no!' but with 'can I have a jacket potato?'

Notes

1 P Storey and R Chamberlin, *Improving the Take-up of Free School Meals*, Department for Education and Employment, 2001
2 Solutions at Work Overview, Iridian Technologies

Eight

The Campaign for Free School Meals in Scotland

John Dickie

'There shall be a Scottish Parliament – I like that.'
Donald Dewar, Scotland's first First Minister

The devolution settlement of 1999 led to responsibility for education, along with health, social justice, and many other key areas of government, coming under the responsibility of a Scottish Parliament for the first time in nearly three hundred years.

With Scotland having some of the highest child poverty rates and worst health inequalities in Europe, the new Scottish Parliament certainly faced a challenge, but it also had an opportunity. One part of this opportunity was to improve the provision of school meals as both a health promoting and an anti-poverty policy measure. Against this background the Campaign for Free School Meals, initiated by CPAG in Scotland, was launched in 2001 to ensure that in post-devolution Scotland every school child could have at least one decent nutritious meal a day.

The School Meals (Scotland) Bill 2002

The Campaign initially focussed on promoting support for a parliamentary Bill to introduce universal free school meals of a minimal nutritional standard. The arguments put forward in favour of free school meals hung on three key themes: reducing stigma, tackling poverty and improving health.

In relation to the first argument there is clear evidence[1] that means-testing creates stigma that discourages take-up of free school meals, with official figures suggesting that around one in three Scots children entitled to free school meals do not take them.[2] Furthermore, for those children who *do* take up their entitlement, evidence suggests that stigma all too often exacerbates the impact of poverty on their vulnerable lives.[3] Given that there is no stigma associated with using NHS hospitals and state schools, there is strong reason to believe that by making free school meals a universal service the stigma too often associated with them can be removed.

Secondly, universal free school meals can help to tackle poverty itself, not just the associated stigma. Currently, a significant number of those children officially living in poverty in Scotland have no right to free school meals, particularly those living in households where parents are working, but on low wages. Extending entitlement to free school meals would help increase the disposable income of some of our poorest households. Furthermore, free meals could play an important role in ensuring that parents are not worse off when moving into work, playing a significant role in supporting the welfare-to-work element of government strategies to end child poverty.

The third argument hinges on the considerable evidence that adequate nutritional standards in school meals could make a significant impact on children's health. Health and nutrition experts have played a key role in the Campaign. They have cited evidence that adult dietary patterns are learnt in childhood, that poor diet in children is linked to disease in later life, that Scottish children eat only two of the five recommended portions of fresh fruit and vegetables a day, and that three-quarters of them appear to eat no green leafy vegetables at all. Free school meals, of a good nutritious standard, have, they argue 'the potential to transform the diet of our young people'.[4] Further evidence suggests that providing nutritious food at school improves cognition, attendance and classroom behaviour, crucial factors in tackling the opportunity gaps disadvantaged children face.[5]

Focusing on these key arguments the Campaign brought together a broad-based coalition of organisations across Scotland, including children's charities, churches, unions, public health groups, anti-poverty groups, dieticians and local government representatives. It encouraged significant debate on school meals in Parliament and beyond, as well as extensive coverage in the Scottish media. However, despite support from across five political parties, Parliament rejected the Bill. The vote against was based largely on the view that money would be better targeted than spent on universal provision. Nevertheless, the argument that increasing access to, and the quality of, school meals could play a significant role in improving health and reducing the impact of poverty on children was widely accepted.

Hungry for Success: the Scottish Executive's response

Despite the failure to introduce universal free school meals, real progress in improving school meals in Scotland has been made. The Scottish Executive (the devolved government for Scotland) Expert Panel on School Meals acknowledged that the 'Bill and subsequent debate were very helpful in raising issues that need to be addressed'. The Expert Panel's final report, *Hungry for Success*, went on to endorse 'the need for nutrient standards and access to free water', and took the view that:

> the Scottish Executive should examine...eligibility to ensure that families and young people do not fall through a gap. The Scottish Executive should reassure themselves that the criteria for eligibility remain appropriate.[6]

In February 2003 The Scottish Executive accepted the recommendations of the Expert Panel in full and committed itself to nutritional standards, free fresh chilled drinking water and healthy meal options in all schools, improving dining halls, raising awareness of free school meal entitlement, ending the advertising of high fat and sugar food and drinks in schools and ensuring schools do 'everything to reduce the stigma often associated with free school meals', particularly through the use of smart card technology.[7]

The principle of universal free provision was accepted – at least to the extent of providing free fruit for all pupils in the first two years of primary schools. Additional resources have been allocated to school meal provision and promotion, and nutrient standards guidance issued to local authorities, schools and caterers. Nutritional analysis software is being developed to assist in meeting these standards. School meals are now to be seen by local authorities as an integral part of education and health strategies, not just as a bolt-on service. Furthermore, monitoring and evaluation arrangements, involving HM Inspectorate of Education, are being put in place to gauge progress in implementing the strategy.

These are significant commitments. However, they are not backed up by statute or regulation. They also fall far short of ensuring all school pupils receive a nutritional meal at least once a day. No extension of free school meal entitlement has been made, despite the significant numbers of poor children who remain excluded and the report's finding that the Executive should 'ensure that families and young people do not fall through a gap'.

Some local authorities have already gone further. In Glasgow (see Chapter 6) the Big Breakfast service provides access to a good-quality, free breakfast for all primary school children. In addition, the governing administration has a manifesto commitment to introduce free school meals for all primary school children by 2007.[8] In Angus, partnership with local fruit producers has led to locally grown strawberries being made available on the school dinner menu, with a resulting substantial increase in school meal consumption.[9] Such developments show what is possible given the political will.

The Campaign goes on...

In March 2004 the Campaign for free school meals was re-launched. At three events in Glasgow, Dundee and Edinburgh, politicians, voluntary sector representatives, young people, health academics and well-known faces, Tam Cowan and Elaine C Smith, put forward the case for free school meals. A new school meals and snacks Bill was drafted and successfully lodged with the Scottish Parliament. Significant media voices are supporting the re-launched Campaign. The *Scottish Daily Mirror* has committed itself, publishing a four-page pull-out highlighting the health and social justice arguments for free school meals.[10] Joanna Blythman, food writer and *Sunday Herald* columnist, has written passionately in support of free school meals, arguing that 'the problem is not that people don't want healthy food...this is not a food issue. It's a poverty issue.'[11]

This time the Bill is framed so as to give powers to ministers to introduce free school lunches for all schoolchildren *or* to target the measure at particular age groups (for example, primary school pupils); those in particular geographic areas (for example, Glasgow); or those in receipt of particular benefits (for example, tax credits); or even just in pilot schools. The aim of this broader approach is to maximise support for extending free school meal entitlement. The Campaign itself remains committed to universal free school meals as a step toward ending stigma, reducing poverty and improving children's health.

Challenges ahead

There are key challenges ahead for those who want to improve access to, and the quality of, school meals in Scotland as a means of tackling poverty and improving health.

First is the need to watch closely the impact of the Scottish Executive's *Hungry for Success* strategy. Are more children taking up their entitlement to free school meals? Have nutrient standards been introduced in all schools? Are children taking up healthy options? Have we seen the end of stigmatisation in the school dinner hall? Have schools stopped advertising junk food and drinks? Much has been left to individual schools and their partners (often facing competing priorities and demands for resources) and progress will need to be closely monitored.

Secondly, it will be necessary to demonstrate that extending free school meal entitlement is actually required if the Scottish Executive's *Hungry for Success* strategy is to be successful. With significant numbers of children who live in poverty excluded from free school meals it is hard to see how 'the criteria for eligibility' referred to by the Expert Panel remain 'appropriate'. Is the Scottish Executive's vision of all Scottish children having access to good-quality nutritious meals at school realisable *without* extending entitlement? Universalism in relation to food at school has already been accepted by the Executive in relation to fruit in primary schools – the next logical step is free school meals for all.

Thirdly, it is vital to demonstrate the link between free school meals and the Westminster and Holyrood strategies to end child poverty by 2020. Increasing the numbers of people in employment lies at the heart of these strategies. Yet evidence from parents themselves highlights the difficulties, disincentives and hardship often caused; moving into low-paid work means losing free school meal entitlement and incurring substantial new expenditure.[12] Free school meals can go a long way toward helping 'make work pay'.

Finally, the debate over children's health has moved on. The need to tackle childhood obesity has become a headline social and political issue.[13] The challenge is now to demonstrate how universal free school meals can play a cost-effective and critical role in fighting the obesity crisis. What better way is there to improve children's diets than to ensure that all children are introduced to good-quality healthy food on a daily basis?

If these challenges can be met, then the day that every Scottish school child, whatever their home circumstances, is guaranteed at least one nutritious meal a day may not be so far off.

Notes

1 P Story and R Chamberlin, *Improving the Take-up of Free School Meals*, Department for Education and Employment, 2001

2 *School Meals in Scotland, January 2004*, Scottish Executive National Statistics, 22 June 2004

3 W McMahon and T Marsh, *Filling the Gap: free school meals, nutrition and poverty*, Child Poverty Action Group, 1999

4 W Wrieden and A S Anderson, 'Nutritional Dimensions of School Meals' in U Brown and D Phillips (eds), *Even the Tatties Have Batter*, CPAG in Scotland, 2002

5 C Ani and S Grantham-McGregor 'The Effects of Breakfast Clubs on Educational Performance, Attendance and Classroom Behaviour' in N Donovan and C Street (eds), *Fit for School*, New Policy Institute, 1999

6 *Hungry for Success: a whole school approach to school meals in Scotland*, Final Report of the Expert Panel on School Meals, Scottish Executive, 2002

7 Scottish Executive Press Release, 19 February 2003

8 *The Glasgow City Council Plan 2003/07*, Glasgow City Council, 2003

9 www.berryscotland.com/events.htm

10 *Scottish Daily Mirror*, 18 March 2004

11 http://www.sspsouthscotland.org.uk/campaigns/freeschoolmeals/ ssv080CP01.php

12 *Our Right to be Heard: lone parents in Scotland speak out*, One Plus, 2004

13 See for example, *Daily Record*, 27 May 2004

Nine
Grab 5! A whole school approach
Kate Bowie and Richard Siddall

Introduction

School meal providers have a challenge – to provide their customers with food that is healthy, low cost and also appealing to a child's taste. Key to a successful meal service is satisfied customers. One way to ensure that customers are satisfied is to involve them in decisions about what food is on offer and how the service is run.

To be a successful school meal service it is therefore essential that all members of the school community are involved in the decision-making process. In order for this to happen, schools need to adopt a 'whole school approach'.

This chapter outlines what is meant by a whole school approach and gives examples of how adopting such an approach can have an impact on school meals. The examples are drawn from schools that have been involved in the Grab 5! project. This is a project run by Sustain, the alliance for better food and farming, for primary schools who want to encourage their children to eat more fruit and vegetables. Over the period of one year, independent evaluation of Grab 5! showed that consumption of fruit and vegetables increased by an average of 30 per cent.

Why a whole school approach?

A whole school approach to improving food and nutrition means:

- engaging everyone in the decisions being made, including children, parents, heads, teachers, governors and catering staff. If everyone is actively engaged, they are more likely to be enthusiastic about changes being made; *and*

• looking at food holistically, including growing, cooking and eating it, considering how nutrition is taught and ensuring that messages being given across the whole school day are consistent.

A whole school approach: the ingredients

The proof is in the policy

An essential element of a whole school approach to improving food and nutrition is a food policy, which provides a framework under which all work on food can fit. A food policy would, for each school, consider food provision (what is being provided and is it appropriate and accessible?), food in the curriculum (how are food issues being taught and does both food provision and extra-curricular activities support this work?) and participation (what structures and systems are in place to ensure that all relevant parties can have a say in the food that the school provides?). The school meal service should be seen as one element within a whole school food policy.

In short, a food policy can help a school offer a range of opportunities for pupils to learn about and experience food which are co-ordinated and which reinforce appropriate messages. They also show a long-term commitment to improving food, nutrition and sustainability.

Students learning about cooking healthy meals

Put all the ideas into a pot and stir

Food projects in schools work best if the plans are made by the school itself. In other words, the school owns the project. This must start with the headteacher. If the head is not fully committed to the work being planned, significant changes, such as in the way the lunchtime service is organised, will not be possible.

Having got the support of the head, everyone else within the school needs to be brought on board. This means talking to them and finding out what they want and how they would like it to happen. Communication may take place at staff/parent/governor meetings, through surveys, in classrooms and assemblies, supported by ad hoc conversations in school corridors and playgrounds. When looking at school meals, meetings involving the school head, the school cook, the area catering manager and a dietician can be very informative and useful. Such meetings bring out people's different views and opinions and can improve understanding of particular circumstances and expectations. School cooks are usually working under very restrictive conditions with tight budgets, limited time, basic equipment and set food items to choose from. Only once these limitations are recognised, can realistic plans for change be made.

Many schools also find a more formal structure a useful mechanism for communication and have set up an action group, often called a school nutrition action group (SNAG). Membership of such a group should include pupils, teachers, parents, caterers, governors, and other key partners such as a school adviser, health promotion adviser, community dietician and school nurse. The group can help develop an ethos of partnership, participation, and ownership within the wider school community. The group could consider many aspects and influences on the school meal service, such as how to:

• improve menus and develop healthy options;
• develop healthy cooking methods;
• encourage the consumption of healthy choices (for example, by training lunchtime supervisors or improving menu information);
• reduce queuing problems;
• improve the dining environment;
• improve customer service;
• ensure meal prices are affordable and do not deter poorer families (those on lower incomes, but who do not qualify for free school meals);
• establish sensible portion sizes;

- improve packed lunches;
- ensure free meal entitlement is known and take-up maximised;
- remove the stigma from pupils taking free school meals; *and*
- teach life skills, including social eating skills and family service.

School councils can also be useful vehicles to engage children and hear their views.

Concoct the perfect plans

Once the school has consulted widely and decided on its priorities, it can start planning. Being realistic about how long it takes to make changes is critical. Convincing children to change their eating habits will not happen overnight. It is vital to think ahead. For example, what will be the cost implications of running regular healthy eating assemblies with the catering providers and how will these costs be met? It is also important for plans to be seen in the context of other work being done around food. If a school wants to encourage more children to take school meals, how can this be done at the same time as promoting healthy eating?

In particular, work should link with and support curriculum work, to maximize learning opportunities and reinforce positive messages. Teachers, for example, may want to run a competition for children to design and make a healthy school meal or look at a particular school meal and explore with the children where the different elements of the meal come from, so creating links with geography. Pupils could also create posters for the dining room promoting 'five a day', reinforcing the healthy eating message at the same time as brightening up the dining room and supporting the art curriculum.

Some tasty recipes

Several schools that were involved in the Grab 5! pilot project found that, even without making any specific changes to the lunchtime menu, an out-come of adopting a whole school approach was that the children started to choose the healthier options. As one school reports:

There has also been a noticeable shift in the children's choice of food at lunchtimes. More children are willing to try food that they have not tasted before and a lot more of them are choosing to eat salad and vegetables. They are also opting for the healthier option desserts.

Some schools took steps to improve the school meal service and lunch menus and found that relatively small changes can have significant impact in terms of take-up of healthier foods. Some examples of work that schools involved in Grab 5! have done include:

- carrying out a survey among children about their views on school meals;
- sending a letter and questionnaire to parents letting them know that the school is looking at school lunches and seeking their opinions;
- inviting the school meal providers to talk to the children about healthy eating and offer samples of the healthier choices;
- inviting a community dietician to talk to the children about healthy eating;
- doing classroom work with children about their favourite healthy lunch;
- inviting parents into school for a free school meal on a particular day, for example during health week;
- investigating the option of offering sandwiches instead of cooked food so that the children on school meals can eat outside during the summer months (lots of schools experience a drop in the number of children eating school meals during the summer as many want to be outside);
- reorganising the seating arrangements so that children taking school meals can sit with their friends with packed lunches;
- offering special theme meals, for example Halloween, Italian or Christmas meals;
- offering fruity milk shakes and smoothies for a small charge (made by children and/or teaching staff); *and*
- printing out large menus and sticking them in windows for parents to see.

One school won an award for improvements made to their lunch service. It now serves healthier meals that are agreed weekly by the school cook and the head, with input from school council. The number of times chips are served in a week has been reduced to just once and water is now served instead of squash. Teachers offer rewards in class to children who choose a healthy lunch and the headteacher and deputy headteacher continue to monitor children's choices. The lunchtime supervisors have been trained to encourage and praise healthy choices.

Another school made changes to the seating arrangements and found that:

> Children can now stay with their friends and this really helps keep numbers. The staff were against the new arrangements at first but now it is quite quick.

Making fruit kebabs is one fun way to learn about healthy eating

Inviting parents for a school meal was also positive:

> Parents were invited to come in and join their children for lunch on certain days and this proved to be a very social occasion with tablecloths, daffodils and music. The parents thoroughly enjoyed this and couldn't believe how good the school meals were. Numbers definitely increased.

As part of the Grab 5! project, training on healthy eating has been provided for school kitchen staff. The events are organised jointly by Grab 5!, the local school meals provider, the Healthy Schools programme and a community dietician. An important aspect of the events is to demonstrate that the role of the catering staff is important, valued and appreciated. This helps foster good relations and a sense of belonging, creating an environment where change is easier to introduce. If properly utilised, the experience and knowledge of school cooks can be invaluable. Below are some of the top tips that kitchen supervisors have come up with on these training events to encourage children to eat school meals and choose the healthier options:

- Make the healthier options look appealing by using garnishes and attractive layout.
- Cut fruit and vegetables into easy, bite-size pieces.
- Offer tasters.
- Add fruit to salads, such as sultanas with grated carrots and apple with celery.
- Disguise fruit and vegetables in popular dishes such as shepherds' pie.
- Talk to the children about the food and the benefits of choosing the healthy options.
- Use rewards for children who try new foods and choose the healthier choices.
- Ensure the dining room areas are attractive, relaxing and user-friendly.
- Invite parents and teaching staff to eat with the children.
- Run special promotions.

For many pupils the midday meal will be the main meal of their day. Its importance cannot be overstated. Experience shows that by adopting a whole school approach to food and making food relevant to everyone in the school, real positive change at lunchtime can be realised.

Part three
Recommendations

Ten
Conclusions and guidelines
Carrieanne Hurley and Ashley Riley

The authors in this book have described their experiences of improving the delivery and quality of school meals. They all show that with dedication and commitment school meals can, and should, be nutritious and healthy, and play a fundamental part in the school day.

Drawing on the various contributions, we make the following key recommendations and suggest some guidelines. They are not always based on scientific research and we hope that they will not stifle other innovative programmes. They do, however, stem from the experience of our authors, from what we have seen in practice, and from what is making a difference.

We continue to campaign for universal free school meals. The recommendations do not undermine this position, but suggest what can be done now to improve our current school meals service.

Political commitment

It is clear from examples in Hull and Glasgow in Chapters 5 and 6 that, in order for school meals to be of high quality, there has to be strong political will and political support in place.

We read of Councillor Colin Inglis in Chapter 5, who experienced strong opposition to his plans. This opposition may often manifest itself in arguments around the potential costs of setting up an improved service and potential cuts in other municipal services, and ignores the costs of not providing a service and the benefits of doing so.

This experience also highlights that for policies or programmes to be effective in the long term, the support of more than one or two individuals within an organisation is required – a point well made by Kate Bowie and Richard Siddall from Sustain in Chapter 9. The examples in *Recipe for Change* often begin with one person; their passion and commitment for school meals has inspired others to support and work with them.

The Government must also take more of a lead and empower authorities to be able to innovate, as we have seen in Hull. It should consider legislating on a number of key aspects of school meal provision, including improving the basic nutritional standards that are currently in place and which only 83 per cent of schools meet every lunchtime.[1] It needs to commit to increasing the budget for school meal provision above inflation every year. In the short term it can act to prevent an estimated £154 million of savings from school meal budgets being used to subsidise other education costs.[2]

Food and nutrition must have a more dominant place within the school curriculum. Where it does, for example in Newham (Chapter 3) and Sunderland (Chapter 7), it makes a difference to what children choose to eat. A recent report from an influential group of cross-party MPs[3] on obesity has also led to a call in the media for more education in schools about food and how it affects children.[4]

Teaching on food and nutrition are not compulsory on the national curriculum, and we suggest that this should be looked at. School governing bodies are permitted to have delegated school meal budgets.[5] Whereas this can allow for innovative projects, such as teaching the importance of nutrition, it can also lead to a lack of expertise on the issue. The most recent Government research has shown that what is being learnt in the classroom is not necessarily being reflected in young people's choices in the canteen, which is an argument for more structured and measurable teaching on nutrition.[6] If the change to the curriculum were made, we hope that commitment to nutrition would be seen across the school so that the risk of effective school meal projects ending when particular members of staff leave would be addressed.

Recommendations

- The Government should make food and nutrition a compulsory part of the national curriculum.
- Basic nutritional standards should be increased from their present basic level.
- All local education authorities should ensure that all their schools have a 'school meals plan' or food policy for the delivery of healthy school meals, together with a minimum requirement for take-up.

Take-up

The importance of take-up has been consistent throughout this book. Over 300,000 children not taking up their free school meal because of a fear of stigmatisation and bullying is not acceptable.[7]

There are a number of ways in which individual schools and local education authorities have attempted to improve take-up. Many of them have had success, such as the retinal scanners introduced by Ed Yeates at the Venerable Bede Secondary School, described in Chapter 7. We want to focus on three. They are achievable, cost effective and, in our experience, make a real difference.

Smart cards

A cashless system, where students carry a form of credit card that holds the cost of their lunch money on its microchip, is often called 'smart cards' and is described in Chapter 4. Schools that use this system, such as in South Gloucestershire, report that take-up increases for all children, including those on free school meals. Money given by the local authority for the cost of free school meals is placed immediately on the student's card by the school without the knowledge of the child's friends or peers. Some schools have taken its development further with great success. Kay Knight describes the reward scheme operating in South Gloucestershire.

A problem that may hinder implementation of a smart card system is the initial layout costs, estimated to be around £3,000 for a whole school. A smart card system, however, saves time previously spent collecting money on a daily basis and brings financial security to schools as no cash is being used.

Views on smart cards do vary and Ed Yeates in Chapter 7 describes the alternative option of iris scanners chosen by his school.

Environment

Glasgow Council has shown in Chapter 6 that the environment in which students have their school dinner is crucial to whether they eat them. Children will not, and do not, eat school meals in what many of us recognise as the traditional school hall canteen. These were often built decades ago and do not reflect the eating environment that young people experience now. In Glasgow and across parts of London, the bright and colour friendly café/fast food/'Fuel Zone' approach is familiar and welcoming to young people and makes a difference to their eating habits.

On a smaller scale, both Newham and South Gloucestershire have shown that small alterations to the environment within existing budgets – redecoration, coloured posters on the wall of the canteen and brighter menus and plates – also make a difference. We know from recent reports on obesity[8] that children visit fast food restaurants on a regular basis. There are lessons we can learn from how the likes of McDonalds and Burger King make their facilities 'child friendly'.

Pupil involvement

A number of schools, such as those in Newham, described in Chapter 3, have introduced SNAGs (school nutritional action groups). These school meals 'committees' comprise students, teachers and representatives from the caterers. SNAGs empower students and give them ownership of school meals. In many areas it is too early to conclude whether or not they are a complete success, but our experience suggests that SNAGs work well and have a positive effect on take-up.

Students are able to inform the caterers of what and how often they want to eat. Caterers are able to inform students of what they can provide within budgets and share new ideas they have for new food products.

SNAGs have no financial setting-up costs but do take time to establish. With commitment from teaching staff and caterers they are making a difference, and are reporting short- and longer-term improvements in the take-up of school meals.

Recommendations

- The Government should introduce 'innovation grants' in order for schools to implement smart card systems.
- Local education authorities must ensure that all schools have a SNAG (school nutritional action group) that includes students and representatives from the school's caterers.

Service

Our experience of meeting catering and teaching staff, and education authorities, suggests that the quality of school meal provision is a widespread concern.

There is a need to train school catering staff, either externally or in-house. Most do not hold a food or cooking qualification and many are paid at minimum wage levels. Conversations with school meal staff often suggest that one reason the job is taken – almost always by women – is because it fits in with their childcare arrangements. Most of the staff do an excellent job, but the growing number of employment agency staff being used suggests that poor pay and poor job prospects means that there is a problem with retention.

We have to recognise that many parents would not allow their child to visit a dentist who had no qualification. School meals are just as important to a child's future health. The London Borough of Newham has introduced NVQ training for its staff, which has been taken up by a number of employees who are staying in their jobs for longer and who have greater job prospects. There is scope for the Government to introduce more apprenticeships.

Healthy food

All of our contributors aim to provide healthy school meals that also appeal to the students.

It is important to keep trying healthy options. When providing healthy food options, Newham works on a '14 hits' strategy. It provides the same healthy option for two weeks (equivalent of a 14-day period). It has found that this is the time it takes to encourage young people to be interested in a food item. Providing a one-off healthy option for one or two days has been found not to work.

The use of fresh ingredients with healthy options does make a difference. For instance, 300,000 portions of fruit are eaten every year in South Gloucestershire (Chapter 4). Our visits to schools across the UK have shown that taking the time to grill and bake food rather than frying makes a major difference to the flavour and nutritional value of the food.

Kay Knight in South Gloucestershire in Chapter 4 and Sustain in Chapter 9 have shown that an approach to healthy food can also include organic food and food grown locally. Both have shown to increase the number of children taking school meals.[9]

Children will therefore choose healthy options when they are provided in a fresh and appealing manner. The experience of our contributors shows this works.

Recommendations

- Catering staff should be valued more highly and have improved pay and conditions.
- All school meals staff should be trained, or receive training, in nutrition, to an agreed national standard.
- Government guidelines for school meals should emphasise the importance of grilling and baking over frying. Only one item of fried food (for example, chips) should be available in one day.

Conclusion

There is much that can be done to improve school meals. *Recipe for Change* can only be a start. There is, of course, much more to be done. The Government must take a more pro-active role to ensure that school children enjoy and benefit from their school meal, and we are encouraged that it has promised to work with us on this.[10]

The Child Poverty Action Group has always argued that school meals play an important role in tackling disadvantage and promoting healthy eating. Our contributors have given us examples of good practice in school meals provision which show the potential for this on the ground. When children eat well, they also do well. The challenge now is for schools, local education authorities and government to ensure that healthy, nutritious school meals, eaten by a high proportion of children, remain high on the agenda. If they do this, we all will benefit.

Notes

1 Food in Schools – a commitment to healthy choice, Press Notice 2004/0135, Department for Education and Skills, 13 July 2004

2 *National School Meals Survey*, Local Authority Catering Alliance, 2003

3 House of Commons Health Select Committee, *Obesity*, Third Report of Session 2003/04 Vol I, 2004

4 'Children's Diets Must Improve', BBC News, 27 May 2004, www.bbc.co.uk

5 http://www.dfes.gov.uk/schoollunches/downloads/PrimaryMain.pdf

6 See note 1

7 P Storey and R Chamberlin, *Improving the Take-up of Free School Meals*, Department for Education and Employment, 2001

8 See note 4

9 *Local Food Works: South Gloucester Council sources local and organic produce for school meals*, Case Study 12, Soil Association, July 2003

10 House of Commons *Hansard*, 27 May 2004, col 1706

Appendix
Useful addresses

BBC News
www.bbc.co.uk/news

CPAG in Scotland
Unit 9, Ladywell
94 Duke Street
Glasgow G4 0UW
Tel: 0141 552 3303
www.cpag.org.uk

Department for Education and Skills
Sanctuary Buildings
Great Smith Street
London SW1P 3BT
www.dfes.gov.uk/school
lunches/juniors.shtml

Department of Health
Richmond House
79 Whitehall
London SW1A 2NL
www.dh.gov.uk/Home/fs/en

Grab 5!
Sustain
94 White Lion Street
London N1 9PF
Tel: 020 7837 1228
www.sustainweb.org/grab5_
index.asp

House of Commons
Westminster
London SW1A OAA
Tel: 020 7219 5466
Email: healthcom@parliament.uk

Iris recognition systems
CRB Solutions
Units 1-8, 32 Dryden Road
Bilston Glen
Loanhead EH20 9LZ
Tel: 0131 440 6100
www.Crbsolutions.co.uk

Iridian Technologies Inc
Tel: 001 856 222 9090
www.iridiantech.com

Local Authority Caterers Association
Bourne House
Horsell Park
Surrey GU21 4LY
Tel: 0148 376 6777
www.laca.co.uk

NCH children's charity
85 Highbury Park
London N5 1UD
Tel: 020 7704 7000
www.nch.org.uk

Scottish Parliament
Edinburgh EH99 1SP
Tel: 0131 348 5000
www.scottish.parliament.uk/
contact.html

Soil Association
Bristol House
40-56 Victoria Street
Bristol BS1 6BY
Tel: 0117 314 5000
www.soilassociation.org.uk

Recipe for Change: a good practice guide to school meals

CHILD POVERTY ACTION GROUP

We are continually on the look out for more examples of good practice in schools and local education authorities or at municipal level.

If you have an example that you think others could benefit from and which you may be willing to share, complete the form below and return to us. Alternatively, please email us the details.

Your name: _____

Your address: _____

_____

Your email: _____

Name of school/authority/group: _____

Address of school/authority/group: _____

_____

Brief description of the good practice: _____

_____

_____

_____

(please continue on a separate sheet if necessary)

Can we contact you to discuss the good practice further?   Yes ☐   No ☐

Can we feature your good practice on the CPAG website?   Yes ☐   No ☐

Return your completed form (we accept photocopies) to:
Ashley Riley
Child Poverty Action Group
94 White Lion Street
London N1 9PF
ariley@cpag.org.uk